LIFE, DEATH, DOG

Between This Pet and the Next

Karen Hansen, PhD

TERRA DONA
- M E D I A -

Published by
Terra Dona Media
23316 NE Redmond-Fall City Rd., Suite 467
Redmond, WA 98053-8376
(206) 538-6564
info@terradonamedia.com

http://www.lifedeathdog.com
http://www.transpersonaltherapy.com
http://www.ourladyfaces.com

Cover artwork: Laura Zion at laurazionartworks@gmail.com
Text and cover design: Bookwrights

ISBN: 978-1-941750-00-1 (Print)
        978-1-94170-01-8 (ebook)
        978-1-94170-02-5 (audio)

Library of Congress Control Number: 2015944223

Publisher's Cataloging-in-Publication data

Hansen, Karen, 1965-
Life , Death , Dog : Between This Pet and the Next / Karen Hansen, PhD.
pages cm
ISBN 978-1-941750-00-1 (pbk)
ISBN 978-1-941750-01-8 (ebook)
ISBN 978-1-941750-02-5 (audio)
Includes bibliographical references.

1. Pet owners --Psychology. 2. Pets --Death --Psychological aspects. 3. Bereavement --Psychological aspects. 4. Grief. I. Title.

SF411.47 H36 2015
    155.9/37 --dc23   ....

Dedication

To all my master therapist dogs, Mitzie, Brewster, Oreo, Coco, Bridget, and Maddie, who have been true healing companions.

ACKNOWLEDGMENTS

It's here, my book has arrived! I wish to thank my editors and helpers: Holly, Carol, Barbara, and Gloria who helped me bring this dog book to life. Thanks also to my family, the many friends, clients and acquaintances who inspired me to write. And special thanks to my husband who tirelessly edited my manuscript and has been my biggest supporter through it all. Many thanks to the therapists that have helped support me on my healing journey over the years. And, of course, great thanks to all the pets. You have touched my life.

CONTENTS

Part III

Part IV

INTRODUCTION

My thoughts, like everybody else's, arise from a personal background and education, but in my case, when thinking about dogs, there is another dimension. Besides being a psychotherapist and coach, I've learned to appreciate dogs in my life as masters of therapy. When I look at my experiences with my one and only treasured four-legged pet and my many part-time pets, there is a lot I've learned that I can translate into my personal life and professional practice. It might sound far-fetched, but I have a picture with the saying, "I don't need therapy, I have a dog!" Not good for business you might say! Seriously, my encounters with dogs and living in close company with them have enriched my life immensely. I am grateful for their presence.

I've learned more about being present as a therapist from dogs than from Carl Rogers, one of the founders of humanistic psychology and a master therapist. In graduate school, I watched a few videos of him practicing unconditional presence. But nothing, save my own healing journey, prepared me for being a therapist as much as what I learned from dogs.

My sister's family dog, Oreo, a black-and-white Havenese, was a prime example of a dog from which I learned much about therapy. I could be having a complete meltdown and he would look me in the eye with a compassion only dogs can muster. At such a time, he never left my side. He stood guard, not sitting in my lap, but staying close enough to let me know he was there, attentive and fully present.

1

Carl Rogers wrote a famous book titled *Person-Centered Therapy*. Oreo effortlessly embodied all three of his person-centered principles: empathy, genuineness and unconditional positive regard. Rogers believed therapists should be warm, authentic and inviting, something dogs do quite naturally. Oreo's book would be titled *Dog-Centered Therapy*. Rogers also wrote another book called *Person to Person: The Problem with Being Human.* That sounds like he was already struggling with having two legs instead of four, so I hope he won't be too offended from the grave, if I measure his method against that of dogs.

In Oreo's approach, as in Roger's, dogs create a comfortable, non-judgmental environment by demonstrating all three principles. The first Rogerian therapy principle, **empathy**, could be seen in Oreo's penetrating eyes. The second principle, **congruence**, was embodied because Oreo couldn't help but be totally real and genuine with people at all times; especially if he knew who was feeding and walking him! Last, the third principle of **unconditional positive regard** is shown in the unconditional love Oreo showers upon his family. Like the Rogerian approach pets also believe in letting others find their own solutions to their problems, a key trait for therapists. Moreover, Oreo's approach and any pet's for that matter, teaches us about the cycle of life, death and rebirth which I discuss later.

As a psychotherapist, I help people deal with grief and take steps toward feeling better. This means that I buy lots of boxes of Kleenex because tissues are a tool of the trade. There have been times in my life where I've gone through a few boxes of Kleenex myself. Being able to grieve is part of life and I can cry buckets with the best of you. I often wonder if that is the reason why women live longer than men. Maybe it isn't because of the genes, DNA, and the like, but simply because we have pre-menstrual syndrome, which means we most likely will lose it at least once in a while. It wasn't until I actually became a therapist and witnessed, day in and day out, all the different ways human beings cope with loss that I realized I'm a big crier. I think I cry more than the average person. I don't know statistically what the average amount of teardrops per person is per year, but I'm sure I must exceed the norm. Maybe I'll live longer because I'm a crier and don't hold things in. I know I'm an intuitive-feeling-type, so maybe that is part of the reason why I'm a crier. It could be the waterworks of middle-age, too, or it could be because I'm getting older or simply that I feel it's OK to cry, because it's a very healthy reaction to both the sorrows and joys of the world. At least, I have my own way of lying down on the couch with a part-time dog and getting some free therapy.

On a personal note, I can tell that I lived for quite a few years as a single woman without husband, partner, or dog, so I understand the single life. Having no pet in the house meant a long time of dreaming what would come first— the husband or the dog. Would I get a ring or a collar?

For a long time, I weighed one against the other, but fate had the last word. As I write this down, I'm happily living with my husband of many years. But the old dream of having a pet is very much still alive. My husband and I don't have kids together, although he does from his previous marriage, but they are adults with their own lives, so the only thing we have to take care of is ourselves, each other, a few plants, and a backyard—a big backyard that in my opinion really needs a dog. Although my husband has soulful eyes and likes to say that I have him on a leash, he doesn't wiggle his tail like a dog!

My hopes and dreams of a dog, though, go further back than the years of my single life. From the time I was born until she died when I was ten, we had a brindle (brown) Boston Terrier, Mitzie, whom my family still keeps alive in many ways. I miss having a dog in the house. There are some pretty big reasons why we haven't got a dog in our household right now, but I don't think I set out to write a book to convince my husband that we need to get a dog, although it seems to have turned out to be an argument, an emotional one at that, that our lives could be much richer and there are strong reasons to consider getting a dog. Upon reflection, though, my writing is more about helping me grieve our family dog. It's wanting to know I did all I can to honor, heal and grieve the loss of Mitzie so that her soul will be free from anything that might have been holding her down here. That would allow me to move on. Move on to what? Another pet? More part-time and rent-a-dogs?

Dreams can help us cope with the loss of a beloved pet. This book first came alive through a series of dreams I had about Mitzie. She had been gone for nearly three decades when the dreams began. The dreams picked up again after we started caring for our neighbor's German Shepherd, Brewster. He also became part of my series of dog memorial dreams. Later, when Brewster's health began to deteriorate, my dreams helped to cope with the upcoming loss. In addition to the dreams came memories long forgotten—sights, smells, sounds and feelings awakened and stirred up deep inside of me.

All these threads are woven in the tapestry of my writing. You can read this book as a diary book, a novel, a memoir, a pet-loss-guide or as a tool for self-discovery in relationship to your pet. As a diary book you can choose random chapters to help you move through your grief. Part four is a toolbox where you will find practical tools, tips and rituals for grieving a pet and moving on. It will help you cope with the loss of a pet and decide where you are between this pet and the next. Some people under-estimate or feel embarrassed or don't understand that mourning a deceased pet is a normal process. You can ponder how your pet has influenced your life or create a spirit packet for your pet, a crying container for yourself and scripts for pet memorials. You'll find questions to ask about putting down a pet, ways to analyze pet dreams, and resources for grief.

I wanted this book to be more than just a series of stories about how I processed the life, death and rebirth of our family dog. I wanted this to be a book of consoling and comfort. So I am going to share my take-away life lessons that I've learned from pets I've loved. Maybe it will help you see your pet with angel wings floating on a cloud, sending love to you from above.

Part I

LIFE

Dogs are Master Therapists

Mitzie as a puppy

"I think dogs are the most amazing creatures; they give unconditional love. For me they are the role model for being alive."

— Gilda Radner

"There's no psychiatrist in the world like a puppy licking your face."

— Ben Williams

"Dogs love their friends and bite their enemies, quite unlike people, who are incapable of pure love and always have to mix love and hate."

— Sigmund Freud

f you have a dog, or if you ever had a dog, or if you like to walk the neighbor's dog, you might have realized that your favorite dog has taught you something. We learn a lot about ourselves in our relationships with human beings. Martin Buber expressed this famously with his adagio "I am becoming myself through you." But in our relationship with animals and, especially, with our pets we can find ourselves just as often reflected in an enlightening manner. Then our pet becomes our teacher.

As a therapist, I have studied many masters of therapy and I have been enriched through my work with clients in the consultation room. My family and friends, my colleagues and co-workers, my fellow travelers and sometimes complete strangers, and, last but not least, my husband have shown me the truth of Buber's "Me and you." But when I started to look back at my experience with pets—in my case mostly dogs—I realized the special bond and important role they have played in my life.

My pets taught me how to live life fully, how to be in the present moment. and the art of living in the now. Their role I deem so important that I like to refer to them as "master therapists," and I'd like to share my learnings from them in a collection of stories. Some tales come from my own life, some I heard from clients, some came in dreams to me. What all these personal stories seem to have in common is an unexpected healing power, the healing power of joy, innocence and love.

Learn something about the pet-centered therapy approach and enjoy a celebration of life as a pet!

Empathy

Dogs are master therapists because they embody empathy. They are completely at home in your universe and communicate with you. It is a moment-to-moment sensitivity that is in the "here and now." It is a sensing of your experience as if it were their own. Dogs live in the present moment and you feel like they get your inner world. Pets go beyond feeling their owners' pain to imitating bodily aches and pains they display. That shows empathy—not the dog's job, of course, but incredible sensitivity, in some manner.

Everyone needs different things during an emotional meltdown. Knowing you are not alone is pretty comforting. Being able to let it all out without fear of judgment or worrying about another being's reactions is, too. Dogs can be more nonjudgmental than humans. Dogs look you in the eye with compassion without flinching. They don't try to talk about it with you; they are just present. Guys always love to try to fix things for women—dogs don't. They just intuit that you need someone to stand by, stand guard, and be present for you.

The other great thing about having a dog is that you may think you're done crying. You look up and he still stands there, hasn't left your side. Maybe you wonder

Master therapist Oreo

why. Suddenly, you start to feel sorry for yourself all over again and another bucket of tears flows and you're glad your dog hasn't left yet. He knows you have crying left to do. He knows better than you how long a crying jag will last! Here is that empathic intuition present again. And after the tears comes the calm, the relief, the peace. Only then does your dog feel like he has done his job and can dismiss himself. When he walks away, you know you're done crying. If you are like me, you're grateful for his quiet, intense, soulful presence. The great empathy take away is, knowing that you're not alone because he is always there for you.

While you're crying, he never stops looking in your eyes. It is like getting to see a reflection of your own soul and the other side through his primal gaze. That is almost unsettling, eerie, in a strange way. Sometimes a dog can make you feel like time has stopped and you are closer to the veil, the other side—heaven. This is often referred to as the luminous realm. To me, it appears that you can see to eternity through those eyes, and somehow that stare is connected to all that ever was or will be. I am usually the one who turns away first.

Through animals like Oreo I've learned that it's okay to cry, and I mean buckets of tears, nonstop and over-flowing. I've learned that if the dog can stand my pain, so can I. Dogs help us go through the pain to reach the other side of grief. They help us feel the relief that comes after the pain.

I have had similar experiences connecting to the heavenly realms when gazing into an infant's eyes. Whether I am gazing at a baby or a dog's eyes I can sense entering that luminous space. What is it about dogs and babies that their long gazes seem to go into infinity and beyond? The primal gaze takes me between chronological and Chiron time; a place beyond clock time where I can be visited by transpersonal realities.

I do open-eye meditations with my husband sometimes and then I don't feel that same urge to break the gaze, but sometimes with dogs and babies, I feel as though if I gaze at them too long, I will get lost in the other side, yearning to get a glimpse of what it is like back "home" again. And by "home" I mean a heavenly home upstairs. I think babies still have glimpses of the blessed place from which they came much better than I as a grown adult. Somewhere, in growing up, I, like most of us have forgotten our home and can only have moments of stolen memory through a dog's or baby's gaze of the great beyond.

Babies haven't been too long down here on earth so they are still connected to heaven upstairs and can take us back to get a glimpse of the divine so easily through an eye meditation. Fresh-born babies don't call it an eye meditation; they are living in the now, so it's just a natural state for them. Some dogs have that same presence. Looking into their eyes, I feel closer to healing spaces and the luminous, heavenly kingdom.

Unconditional love is a lot like unconditional positive regard, Carl Rogers's third good therapist principle. It's all the same. It's being loved no matter who you are, where you come from, or what you do or don't do. It's unconditional because there are no strings attached. It's love for simply just being. James Baraz in his book *Awakening Joy*[1] shares some wisdom he learned from Ram Dass. Dass speaks of awakening love, suggesting that it is never lost since it's always been there just waiting to be set in motion. Through unwavering empathy dogs are catalysts to bring love into our lives awakening unconditional love inside of us.

Genuineness

In our family, unconditional love came in the package of Boston Terriers. The Boston mania started back when I was

Look at that brindle coat!

a little girl. My mother always told me stories about her aunt's Boston Terrier named Mickey, who lived with her, her siblings, and her mother in the 1940s. Well-trained, Mickey knew to stop and sit at stop lights. He could heel, roll over, and do other tricks. Mickey is what I call a "rent-a-dog." When my mother was five, her father died. Her aunt brought her dog Mickey over to their house to help cope with the tragic loss; hence, Mickey became the family's first rent-a-dog—and a precious one at that. So "dogs = comfort" is a family trait. A tradition is more like it.

It's because of Mickey that my mother wanted to get a Boston Terrier dog for her family of her own someday.

And my mom got her brown, Boston Terrier, Mitzie from the Bolton farm not far from where she grew up in the Midwest, which makes her even more connected to memories of comfort, family and roots. Grandpa A. had heard that there were some puppies left in the farm litter. Mitzie was eight weeks old when they got her and they paid $15.

She was born in May and was officially seven-eighths Boston Terrier and the only brindle in the litter. Her sister came down on the train a few weeks later after a neighbor was so smitten with Mitzie that they wanted a Boston Terrier themselves from the same litter.

She was everyone's dog, but Mitzie was always first and foremost mom's dog. So it must have been a shock to Mitzie when I came on the scene much like it is for any sibling to have a new baby sister. Mitzie had quite a reaction when my parents first brought me home from the hospital. She reportedly shook when they laid me in the crib in the living room. She didn't know what to make of this new little being coming into her inner pack. Maybe she sensed that she would not have as much of Mom's attention in the coming months—or maybe she intuitively knew at some point in my younger days, I would pull her tail! I upset the order of things in her world, that's for sure. She loved me, nonetheless. She was three when I was born, gentle and loving with me as most dogs are around little ones. At least that is what I believe and have been told.

Dogs are just here to remind us to unconditionally love ourselves. Mitzie embodied Carl Roger's principle by showering us with unconditional love. She didn't care if I was happy or sad, good enough or smart enough. She didn't care what I looked like, if I did poorly on a test, fought with a friend. She just loved me no matter what. And she was there being genuine just by her presence or by looking me in the eye reassuring and soothing. I could pet her whenever I was having a bad day.

Dogs are a benevolent presence that can tenderly hold our losses. They stand by us when we grieving. They remind us that everything is okay and they never judge us. Tenderness is a quality that pets bring into our lives when we most need it.

One reason I often love to get up early and greet the day is because it reminds me of rising at dawn as a child and sitting with our dog. In the quiet of the morning, I would find her and she would always be there for me.

My mother would rise, too, and pour me a glass of juice and then go back to bed. At first it was grape juice, but my lip swelled up from the grapes so she switched to Hawaiian punch. I would create my own little cubbyhole beside the television with the floor heater behind me and Mitzie asleep to my left. She had her spot in her orange bed underneath the built-in bookshelf. She was often still sleeping but didn't seem to mind if I petted her a bit. She would curl up in a ball, slowly raise her head, smile at me, then go back to sleep. Or sometimes she would just sit there and beam her love at me.

My mother said that Mickey would run into their room in the morning and jump up on top of the beds and wake up her and her sister. I now see how I was lucky like Mom to have a brindle Boston Terrier greet me in the morning. While Mitzie didn't run into my room to wake me up, she was by the heater every morning. Dogs are family comforters providing connection and love. When I started to watch rent-a-dog Brewster for our neighbors, I was reminded of how much I love to have a dog with me to start my day. I couldn't wait to go over to the garage and greet him in the morning. I would sit on a mat beside him and soak up that look a dog first gives you in the morning. Some are lazy like Mitzie and just sleep on; others like Oreo will rise to greet the day with you even if their arthritis is slowing them down. Brewster couldn't wait to go outside with you to get the morning paper. It's been different with every dog, but like Ram Dass says, the love is always waiting for you; it is never lost.

Unconditional Positive Regard

Isn't having a pet cheaper than therapy? I told you, the saying goes, *I don't need therapy, I have a dog.* Dogs can console like only dogs can. They are genuine in that they are made for comforting. So our poor dog had the job of being the family comforter. It sounds like I'm talking about some family quilt, the comforter, passed down from the generations. But that is what my parents did. They created a home with a loving dog because they knew about the unconditional love dogs provide. Maybe parents instinctively know that they won't always be physically or emotionally present for their children and get a dog to help fill the voids in life.

Some of that comforting principle has continued down through the generations. Our dog wouldn't sit and look us in the eye like Oreo, but she would also never leave our sides, either. I often thought at the end of her thirteen years, when she suffered heart problems, it might have been because she had held the family's pain so well—too well, in fact—that her heart gave out. Our family has immortalized her in a way. At Christmas, tokens of her often appear in stockings and wrappings, reminding us of her love.

When my parents got Mitzie as a puppy from the farm in Minnesota, they picked her out because she was friendly and had a beautiful brindle coat. The Boston Terrier, Mickey, that I mentioned earlier who watched over my mother after her father died, had a beautiful brindle coat, too, which is why they picked her from the litter. Mitzie had adorable white socks and perfect little ears and tail.

She was well trained and could sit, stay, heel, and dance for a treat. She bit me once only but didn't break skin—and I deserved it for pulling her tail! She loved lying in the sun, sitting next to the heater, riding in Mom's bike basket, riding in the car, and playing tug of war with her toys. Like most dogs, she hated vet visits, fireworks, and family vacations that didn't include her. She was always

there at the door to greet us and was everybody's confi-
dante.

Twenty years after Mitzie's death, I gave everyone
in my family an ornament depicting our breed of dog
with wings; finally, Mitzie is home to heaven where she
belongs. We all laughed until we cried when those ornaments appeared out of their boxes. It's good we can see
the humor in how we have let Mitzie's memory live on;
perhaps letting her linger longer, preserved beyond her
expiration date. Nevertheless, I get a kick out of putting
her on the Christmas tree every year.

Dogs can console and act as master therapists. I have
even met some dogs that act as great couples' therapists. For
example, my colleague Melissa and her husband might be
having a discussion, they don't really call it an argument,
it's just a discussion. And Melissa will say to her husband,
"Are you mad," He responds, "No, No, I'm not mad, I'm
fine. I'm really fine." But that isn't really the case because
Claudia, their dog who isn't even in the room during the
discussion, will come downstairs and be all over her husband. She will be crawling up on him and licking him.
She won't leave him alone saying to him, "You're really
mad, you're really upset aren't you."

You can't fool Claudia. She is a bono fide couples' therapist. She can see right through the couple when they are
angry and not admitting it to each other. And she can
see through their children's tears as to whether they are
authentic or not. Once, when one of the children was upset about something and started crying in a corner, Claudia was right there by her side comforting her. But, there
were other times when her children would fake cry. For
instance, when her daughter was upset because she wasn't
allowed to go over and play at her friend's house and
went then to the same corner and started to pretend to
cry, Claudia would just ignore her. She knew she was only
pretending and wouldn't go over to comfort her. Claudia
knew the difference between authentic crying and ma-

nipulative crying. That dog is not only a skilled couples' therapist, but can work with children as well!

First Mitzie Dream

I had a number of Mitzie dreams over the last decade. Those dreams played an important role in healing the loss of Mitzie. In addition, memories and, what in Jungian psychology would be called "active imagination," appeared during that same period when I was grieving Mitzie's death as an adult aspiring to honor her fully. Because I associate dogs with the dawn of the day it fits that she would appear to me early one morning in a kind of lucid dream state or misty vision. I've called it *"Mitzie in the Forest."*

I am leaning against a tree in a forest shortly after dawn. The mist is still rising from the ground and the forest smells of fresh pine. In my imagination, I can see her running down the forest floor, flying over the stump, so happy to see me. I can feel her short, brindle hairs like stubble as they brush against my hand. She smells like Mitzie—the smell I caught a whiff of when I sat by her bed. I can see her long tongue hanging out as she pants on a hot summer's day.

Mitzie on a hot day

It was a surprise to imagine her in this environment. I only have memories of her from times growing up. She looked like a fish out of water here in the deep forest of my imagination. Compared to our crisp, tightly groomed lawn where I grew up, the forest was quite the shock for her. In contrast to this rich, private forest full of trees where I was meditating, in Mitzie's suburban world where I grew up, our backyard had few trees and some bushes stood as a border between us and our neighbors. There was no forest of tall trees around our home in the Midwest like we have here in the Pacific Northwest. She would be in a whole new world, one where she could run, sniff, and explore in utter and complete joy. It's more a forest for big dogs, though if she were living today with us, how could we protect her from coyotes, bears and others animals that roam here? According to the Animal Control and Wildlife services in our county, coyotes will go after any pet under 16 pounds. Yikes, Mitzie was a small dog and under sixteen pounds! Good thing I don't have to worry about her in real life because this all happened in my imagination.

This picture of Mitzie running to greet me in the forest takes me back to my memories as a child when she rose to greet me in the morning, dozing in her plastic make-shift orange bed. I was content as a child, too, with just the dog, juice, heater, and Ray Rayner on TV. Rising early is like the gift that keeps on giving. Even though Mitzie is no longer with me to greet the morning, a part of my inner child still waits patiently, it seems, for her to come around the corner. Of course, I know she never will, but my mind's eye sees her—or maybe it's the spirits of the forest imposing an impression, a psychic impression much like a hand that has been lifted out of the sand leaves an imprint. So, too, does the image of her bounding down the forest path to greet me with the rising dawn leave its own imprint in my subconscious. It is lonely sometimes in the early dawn without her presence and affections. To just be near her again would soothe the soul. Almost as if by magic, this holographic image appearing to me is a very close second to feeling near her again.

Morning has always been a magical time of day for me. It started as a toddler rising early with Mitzie, savoring every still moment until the sun rose. I still feel the same magic today when I rise early. I first hear the sound of the frogs and then a quiet pause followed by more frogs. Then I hear the chirp of a distant solo bird increasing in volume. Others join her chorus until the whole forest is a symphony of their song to meet the day.

That's when I saw Mitzie's impression. No physical form—only the feeling or imagining of her coming down to greet me. The sky was still a grey darkness, slowly fading with the coming light. I imagined reaching out to pet her. I still miss her, especially if I have had a bad day, but now she has appeared as a sign that she appreciates my genuine attempt to grieve and honor her.

Part-Time Pets are the Best

Best dog book!

I've been lucky enough to have many part-time master therapist pets, mostly dogs (see back of the book for a list of the cast of characters). Since my single lifestyle didn't seem right for a dog, I quickly grew attached to my part-time pets. One of my favorite storybooks growing up was Part-Time Dog by Jane Thayer. It's about a little long-haired Dachshund, Brownie, who wants to find the perfect home. He doesn't belong to anyone, and three different neighbors feed and let him sleep in their houses. Brownie didn't have an official home on Maple Street. I think that could have been the best of all worlds when I was single, I would have loved to have shared ownership of a dog. It reminds me of the book *It Takes a Village* about needed extra familial and community supports to raise a child. Similarly, it could take a neighborhood to raise a dog. Often times we live far away from our families and don't have someone to watch the dog. A neighbor girl down the street took great care of Mitzie when we were on vacation.

Fast-forward twenty-plus years and, as adults, my husband and I took care of one of our neighbors' dog, Brewster, a German Shepard. Taking care of him reminded me of the above book I read as child. Brewster was a classic part-time dog. After we watched him for a month, I cried when he went home and called the owners up that week to ask to continue taking him for walks. We started watching him over the next few years. The attachment grew slowly over time and began with giving him bones. This gradually evolved into taking him for walks around our block. I knew I was bonding and that he was 14-years-old. His hips went out sometimes when he tried to stand. He was my buddy and I loved taking care of him.

Sharply around five or so, he would wander over to our house when his owners went in for dinner. If it was a nice summer's night, we sat outside on the lawn with him during the evening hours. He would already have had a sip of his owner's beer after his workday next door, so he came over to our house for appetizers.

I treasure those peaceful quiet nights with our part-time dog. When it was dark, he would go home through his doggie-door in his garage and later make his rounds of not only his own yard but ours as well. Sometimes, he might come by again to see if we were in the hot tub where he knew we were good for another treat. I swear I can sometimes hear the jingle of his collar even though he has been gone for years now.

I have a favorite Brewster memory of coming up our long driveway on a quiet summer's evening. As I came up the hill, I saw my husband peacefully lounging in the sun in our yard with Brewster sitting in the grass to his left. I thought to myself how lucky I was coming home to these two guys. I happily joined them, bringing a treat, my half of Brewster's bone. Since he wasn't our dog, we didn't want to spoil him too badly, so we split and gave him half a bone in the morning and half in the early evening.

My mom had part-time and rent-a-dogs, too. My parent's rent-a-dog program started after we had moved out of the family house.

Porter came later into my parents' life, a gem of a black Lab. His owner often took Porter to work in the back of his pickup. On the days Porter stayed home, though, he walked with my parents. His owner told my parents they could walk him whenever they wanted. Everybody wins with a rent-a-dog. The renters get all the benefits of having a dog and all, dog and humans, get fresh air and exercise.

Cooper, my mom's neighbor's dog

The first rent-a-dog was Cooper, a Golden Labrador and German Shepherd mix. When the next-door neighbors got him, they chained him up beside my parents' bedroom window. My mother got understandably annoyed because he barked non-stop every morning at dawn.

Finally, she had had it and went over and asked if she could walk the dog while everyone was at work. Cooper's mom was a single parent with four kids so she appreciated the help. So Mom took Cooper—or more like he took her—down to the park every morning. Once he had his walk, he was good the whole day and never barked at all. He always knew when Mom got up and would whine a bit if she didn't walk him first thing.

Next thing you know, the dog was in the house, was best buddies with my dad, and went to the cabin on weekends—even rode in the boat. At the cabin, Cooper stayed in the garage, and just so he wouldn't get too lonely, my mother took part of the Sunday paper and read it in the garage with him at her feet. They even had a heater cranked up for Cooper on cool nights. Cooper was spoiled and got to eat a pancake on Sunday morning along with his real dog food. Feeding a dog a pancake is a bit of a family tradition, too, as you will read later. I will tell you in a moment. As of this writing my mother is looking for another part-time dog. She recently joked with a neighbor that if they ever needed a dog sitter to let her know. "I have references," she said smiling referring of course to Porter and Cooper!

Oscar

This is Oscar, my rent-a-bird. I know this is a book about dogs, but it wouldn't be complete without telling you about my rent-a-bird, who also taught me a thing or two about not judging a pet type before you've tried it. Oscar showed me about the journey from life to death and pet visitations. Oscar was my dear friend and roommate's parakeet. Up to that point, I did not love birds and thought pet birds were a nuisance. That all changed with Oscar.

He loved to fly around the room and sit on people's heads. The first time he flew on mine, I nearly screamed. It wasn't long before his yellow spotted wings grew on me and I thought of him as my new-found rent-a-pet bird. His chirping music filled our apartment and lifted my spirits. I became quite attached to the bird that let me love him. He would often fly over when I was meditating. If I had a bad day or was upset about something he would fly over to comfort me. Looking back, I remember how much better I felt when he was in the room with me, especially when he flew over and just sat on my head. All my burdens fell away and my energy lifted. My head felt lighter. He was doing his form of bird Reiki, rebalancing my chakras for me! Whether a pet is singing, snoring, yawning or walking, or you hear the jingle of their collar, all those sounds are grounding and bring a sense of comfort and routine to the day.

Pancakes

Perhaps part-time dogs run in the family. Maybe that is why my mother bought us the *Part-Time Dog* book in the first place. She is a lover of all things "nature." She will tend to stray dogs, lovingly care for her flowers, feed the birds, and pay attention to every plant in her garden. I joke that she is part fairy and that I have inherited that streak from her.

Shep, my mother's farm dog

Mothers and daughters follow each other's paths and leads. You learn about life from both of your parents. I'm just like my mother when it comes to adopting part-time dogs. I take home lost dogs, adopt part-time dogs, and feed my inner child through dog encounters. We are different in that Mom is also a cat lover. I am more fond of dogs than cats.

Mom speaks of having tamed all the kittens on the farm where she grew up. She would have had cats in the house if my father and I had not been allergic to them.

Mom's family had a farm dog named Shep, who helped round up the cows, and Buster, a short, black-haired mutt. Later came Bernie, a Saint Bernard who was more of her brother's buddy.

Mom's mother would make extra pancakes to feed the dogs every morning. On Sunday evenings at home, we often had pancakes or waffles for dinner, reminiscent of Mom having pancakes on the farm.

Two stray dogs came around my parents' home one cold winter Sunday afternoon and she fed them pancakes too. They wouldn't let them in the house, so my parents got a big cardboard box and put a blanket in it for the dogs to sleep in that night as it was too cold for them without any cover. They were long gone in the morning. My mother had her own powerful encounters with dogs that brought comfort. Food, family and pancakes is a theme that followed her from childhood to adulthood and into the mouths of her part-time dogs. It will come as no surprise that one of the ways I nurture those I love is by making pancakes.

Some dogs aren't meant to be adopted. Each has its own purpose in life. These guys seemed to be on the move and liked their freedom. Maybe they were on the run from animal control. Full-time and part-time and rent-a-dogs can come and go in our lives at any time. It's best to find ways to let them go and remember we all have our own path in life. We don't really need to analyze how and why a dog has come into our lives, just be with it.

Being a dog lover I welcome friendly dog encounters. Dogs run loose a lot in our neighborhood of forest and trees. I wonder if the big dogs have gotten loose because of being tormented by a coyote. When I'm driving and I see dogs running in the street, I pull over and wait to make sure they are out of harm's way. When my husband and I are out walking, we sometimes have dogs follow us who appear to be lost. Naturally, I am looking for the jingle of a collar and wondering where home is for them. "Don't pay them attention or they will really follow us all the way home," my husband has said on these encounters. I usually am checking over my shoulder to see if they turn around and really know where home is. Once a dog walked all the way home with us and up our driveway. He had a tag so I called and his owner came over awhile later to get him. The dog was thirsty and we fed him some of Brewster's bones. I secretly hoped of course, that maybe, just maybe, his owner wouldn't be home for awhile and would ask us to keep him for the day! But that didn't happen, alas!

Grounding With Your Pets

Walking is grounding. Dogs give us that gift. Maybe that is because they are a part of the animal kingdom, grounded to Mother Earth and more deeply in tune with her rhythms and her flow to heaven. I feel like dogs ground me when I need it the most. Maybe it's because they have four legs instead of our two, connecting us to the earth with every step taken. Or maybe it's because they really take the time to smell the fresh air. I'm more likely to walk if I have a dog in my life, hence, I would feel more grounded.

In the mornings, I walked Brewster to get our newspaper, and, like a good German Shepherd knows how, he just loved to stand in the early light, the dew still glistening on the ground, the sensation of the fresh air tingling the skin—or fur, in his case. And he drank it all up through his nose.

We never just stopped at getting the paper; he always had to turn the corner to greet the day, facing the sun rising in the east, sniffing all the way. I would gladly go with him because I felt so alive in those moments. He would pause as if time had stopped, and because of his earthy nature, I stopped and smelled the roses, too. Having a dog is equivalent to walking around the earth barefoot every day. The Earth provides natural electric conductivity and animals do, too. A dog like Brewster can ground you all day long.

Bridget and Author

Another favorite rent-a-dog was Bridget, a sweet yellow Lab. Long ago she belonged to my boyfriend's parents. When he moved out-of-state for a new job, they were kind enough to loan me Bridget for a few weeks to help ease the loss.

Bridget was only too happy to be of help. She was getting on in her years, cheerful, playful, and obedient. She was probably the first to incline me toward larger dogs. She didn't need a leash and loved to walk. I lived in a rental on a ten-acre former sheep farm, so she had plenty of room to roam. My neighbors were kind enough to take her out on the evenings I worked, and she had an old, pink comforter next to the woodstove as her station. It was wintertime, and we took long walks with the snow falling up the mountaintops of Vermont. It was fun! I loved to take her out while hiking and those were glorious days. Talk about grounding. It doesn't get better than walking in the green mountains of Vermont with a beauty like Bridget! She loved to ride in the back seat of my car and was always ready for action.

Bridget wasn't allowed upstairs in the office or bedroom of my apartment and that seemed to work for both of us, but she came to my rescue one evening when I was upstairs alone and the power went out. I remember panicking a bit without a flashlight in the pitch black dark. I called to Bridget, and even though she was arthritic and knew she wasn't technically allowed upstairs and never had been there, I quickly heard her collar jingling, signaling that she was on her way. I couldn't see her, but she found me and came right up to keep me company in the dark. I found a candle to light, but her warm fur next to me had never felt better than on that night. I've learned that dogs can ground and provide that feeling of safety in many a situation. They can restore a lost connection to nature, which helps brings us back to the center of ourselves.

I laughed at seeing her get up to greet the morning. She loved to just stand outside on my lawn and sniff the dew. I lived on a quiet country road; nevertheless, there was traffic and she was oblivious to it when it came to parking herself right in the middle of the road to smell the fresh air. I found her one morning out there and a car had stopped for her, and she just didn't get it that she might be in the way. I shouldn't have let her stand in the road.

Supposedly, Labradors are alert, active, and intelligent; however, some people think that they are not the smartest dogs in the world because they have been carelessly overbred. Bridget certainly wasn't the smartest, part-time dog I've ever known, but she was definitely one of the most lovable, and that's what I remember most about her. But she just didn't get it that she didn't own the morning road, and it made me nervous, especially since she was a rent-a-dog and I wanted to take good care of her. *Bridget, get out of the way of oncoming traffic!* That was her way of grounding and starting her day. She wouldn't budge from what she saw as her morning sniffing station. I had to take the dog out and that got me out in the fresh air and outdoors, which is grounding in itself, I told you. Once again, that's one of the benefits of a having a dog!

Another rent-a-dog was Jazz, a black Lab, belonging to my friend whose office was next door to mine when I started my first psychotherapy practice. Jazz was ready to take a walk with me any time. We circled down through town to the lake, where, if it was warm enough, she took a short swim. Jazz was a great buddy and helped me to restore and recharge in between seeing clients. Dogs have a way of doing that, I believe. Jazz really grounded me, was fun, affectionate, and the perfect, walking, rent-a-dog for me. Jazz brought a steady, secure presence to my everyday routine during that time.

I once was called to a hospital after a client attempted-suicide. She was a dog lover and we had her pull a picture of her dog up on her phone as a way to ground her to this world. Spontaneously, her loved ones and I formed a circle around her hospital bed and sent her good thoughts for a speedy recovery. Through the picture, her pet was a part of that circle, too.

Intuition and Pets

Pets are so intuitive. Once, when I visited Oreo's home, he knew I had food poisoning before I did. I remember feeling a little off as I headed into the bathroom and wondered why he followed me. *Couldn't I have a little privacy?* Then my head started to spin and I nearly swooned and passed out. I realized Oreo knew what was going to happen even before I did. He kept vigil along with my family while I lay sick for the next forty-eight hours. He came in to check on me from time to time like a good watch dog because he considered me one of his pack.

Oreo passed away at only ten years of age. "I know you're out there somewhere, Oreo." That is the song that comes to my mind when I fondly think of him. Some dogs are natural counselors and he was one of them. Dogs are "pack" animals, and I was lucky to be included in on Oreo's pack of four- and two-legged species.

I never knew I was going to have some therapy sessions when I went to visit Oreo's home. But alas, there he was, my own personal Carl Rogers, looking me in the eye. It was just like the videos I watched of the master at work. And I could have all the air time I wanted to talk and he patiently listened. He didn't roll his eyes or look at the clock on the wall, and I didn't even have to talk because he was telepathic. His ears heard everything even in the silence. And he couldn't talk back, so I had no worries that he would be like a certain TV psychologist who gives too much advice about how to live your life.

Pets teach us about our intuition. We can find our own answers when using the dog-centered approach. And it's free. We all know therapy can be expensive (but well worth it!). There is no diagnosis code or complex attached to it, either. No one has to mess with insurance premiums!

I don't know if I would call it intuition but I happen to be out and about seeing Boston Terriers on the make ever since I started this book. Maybe it is more like synchronicity. All of the sudden one just showed up on our dead end street one day. I like to call this a 'dog clue.' Dolly Parton in her book, *Dream More: Celebrate the Dreamer in You*, shares what she calls 'God clues' or signs. When she has a decision to make and doesn't know what to do she waits for her inner knowing "God clues." It's a spiritual center that she calls her "God core." This center is a place where heaven and earth meet. When she doesn't know her next step, she will wait for it to be revealed often in strange and mysterious ways.

I think running into these Boston Terriers all over the city have been my "dog clues" that I needed to keep going on with this dog book. Our pets are like an inner connection. They encourage us to daydream as we pet their fur or as they snuggle next to our leg. It is soothing, comforting like a blanket. Pets can take us to an inner place no human can. When we are busy running around and forget to just be, a pet can help us to remember to take a moment and just be. Husbands, partners, kids they all can take us out of that inner connection. Pets, since they can't talk, are less likely to and that is why they connect us to our intuition.

Laughter is the Best Medicine

Dogs must know when you really need a good laugh. I can't count the number of times I've been in tears laughing from a dog's antics. The funniest part is that they don't even know they are trying to be funny. I will share a few comedy scenes from dogs I loved. The first that comes to my mind is watching Dash stick his nose out of the window when driving, giving his a wind-blown hairdo. I always love seeing dogs having their hair done!

Another memory is watching Oreo sleep on his back with his little hind paws up in the air. What a hoot. He was the loudest snoring dog ever! He sacked out on the edge of the leather couch and snoozed away. But with every snooze, his legs shook along with his head. Once he must have been dreaming, because his restless legs moved so fast and furiously as if he were running upside down on his back. As he twisted his back against the couch, you could hear little grunts and groans as his legs moved in sync with his snores.

The third story is really hilarious, I think. When Oreo and his brother Dash met my husband for the first time, they generously welcomed him into their pack. Later, though, when we were getting ready to leave, my husband put on his Indiana Jones hat. Everything changed. They both looked up at him. Only a minute before, they had gazed at him with adoration and love, but now they growled! He took off the hat and they wagged their tails. He put it on and they growled. He took it off again, and they wagged their tails. It gave a whole new meaning to "near-sightedness." We all laughed at their antics and we left the house the way they wanted him to, without the hat on.

Then there was Kaylee, the best and funniest dog. She was a little, gray Scottish Terrier with a lot of spunk, independence, and an "I can do whatever I want" attitude. She was also a bit of a princess and she knew it. She was getting on in years. On one of my visits, she found her way into my travel bag where I had some left-over chocolate protein powder. Luckily, it wasn't a full serving, because we know how dangerous chocolate is for dogs! She strutted out of my room into the hall with a brown mustache of powder over the lip of her mouth. She suddenly wasn't a girl dog anymore but a gray-haired old man! Those dogs already look like they have a mustache, but against her gray hair, it was so striking and looked so real—almost as though she had put on a Halloween costume and was waiting for trick-or-treaters. I never dog-watched Kaylee, but she was a spitfire and a love all the same, so I consider her an honorary rent-a-dog.

Sweet Sophie

The last comedy I share is a test of puppy love. I was visiting my sister and we had planned that I would be house-and pet-sitting for her. Hence, I was really a guest in Sophie's family. Sweet Sophie is a Havenese puppy and is, for all measure, a really easy dog. I was so excited to finally meet her. She had recently lost her older brother, Dash, to cancer and was having a hard time getting the hang of potty training. An illness in the family prevented them from ensuring she was trained to go outside early on; hence, the puppy pee pads in the guest bathroom. Their home has a sliding door that separates the guest room and across-the-hall bathroom from the rest of the house. Of all places, that was her station to pee and poop. There were other pads in the master bathroom, but this was her favorite place to pee. I didn't even know they sold such a thing! Disposable pet pads have replaced the old a newspaper-at-the-door trick.

What is the dog psychology of sharing a bathroom? This, by all accounts, was her bathroom and I was intruding on her space. When I went into the bathroom, Sophie followed and went, too! At first, I thought this was hilarious! After the first day or two, I said to myself, "This is not right. You are not human. You need to go outside!" It didn't take long for me to start analyzing the puppy psychology of sharing the bathroom with Sophie.

It got to the point where if I had to go, I first took her outside to see if she'd do her thing. She usually wouldn't! I would go into the bathroom and shut the door for privacy. Sure enough, she'd soon be scratching at the door. I would come out and she would go in and pee on her little pee pad. With her eyes, Sophie seemed to be saying, "You're doing it in the bathroom. Why can't I? What's the big deal? I've been trained to pee like a human and now I have to share my bathroom with you."

She was so sweet and innocent-looking that I don't think she felt that put-out by sharing. It was the whole idea that I thought she would actually go outside that threw her. A few times, the puppy training actually worked! But later in the day, especially if I was gone for a while, she'd be back on the pad.

She never went in her crate where she slept, however. When I woke late that Sunday morning, I went to the bathroom while I left her in her crate. But she must have heard me, because when I immediately took her outside, she wouldn't go. Instead, after holding it all morning, she proceeded to follow me into the bathroom and pee on the pad while I brushed my teeth!

When Sophie's parents came home and their master bathroom pee pad was available, she still preferred mine. By this time, we had bonded in the bathroom, and I just accepted that she was sharing *her* bathroom with me. *I*, after all, was the guest!

Still it had to be confusing for poor Sophie, and I trusted she would slowly make her way from the pee pad being moved to the door to the grass outside for her business. While I loved my time with Sophie and found the bathroom sharing arrangement hilarious, staying with Sophie really made me think twice about getting a dog and having to put in the time and energy to potty train.

Healing Spaces

I have learned from dogs something about holding space for others. It takes a special kind of dog or person, for that matter, to be able to sit through other people's meltdowns. I do it all the time as a therapist. I consider it a privilege to do the work I do. I also know something about meltdowns, because I've had plenty of good ones in my life. I know what it feels like to grieve, release, and let go. Pets help us to grieve openly and are comforting. They stabilize us so we can say yes to a life full of change, impermanence, and loss.

Mitzie at her best

In popular psychology, we all have an inner child, a child-like aspect that may have emotional wounds, such as abandonment, that need to be processsed. Jung talked about the innocence of the inner child and suggested that an aspect of the inner child can be dependent, abandoned, divine, magical and or a wonder child. When doing inner child work with clients, I have found it can be helpful in the process to find an inner resource, a symbol of the inner child—maybe a picture, or object, or even an experience. This inner resource can be a peaceful place, a nurturing figure, or a protective figure. Inner resources create a container, a holding space of comfort and reassurance. Pets are master therapists when it comes to creating inner and outer resources for the child-like parts of us all.

Madeline came in to work with a broken heart and traced it back to grieving losses as a foster child. I gave her the homework of finding an inner resource connected to her inner child. She came back the next week telling me about how she had seen an ad for a local dog show that week. She spontaneously decided to go even though she had cats and no desire to add a dog to the mix. As a foster child, she had experienced great love and warmth from dogs in foster homes. "It really brought out the little kid in me. It was so fun to go around and look at all the different kinds of dogs I remembered being around as a kid."

She loved her cats but said there was something special about dogs that reconnected her to her inner child. It was a way for her to nurture and care for that younger part of herself. And she reported, "It was really fun to talk to the dog owners."

Dogs can be used as protective inner resources when doing subconscious therapeutic work. Sometimes clients choose their dogs as nurturing or protective figures. In my work with Eye Movement Desensitization and Reprocessing (EMDR), I develop an anchor resource with every client. They then recall disturbing images while receiving one of several types of bilateral sensory input, including side-to-side eye movements. The therapy is actually re-sourcing with bi-lateral stimulation. The tapping-in of the inner resource lays down new neuropathways that a client can use on his or her own out of the office.

This resourcing work can be a helpful adjunct in therapy. Bi-lateral stimulation through the eyes or tapping the knee or shoulder is used to anchor the resource of comfort or support. Clients can still imagine what they need. For example, a comfortable and soothing presence like a dog can be tapped in when a client was alone as a child. If clients can imagine it, they can tap into their pet resource. This potential self-soothing technique is available for all and all kinds of animals can be protectors for clients. Power animals, such as deer, bears, and eagles, have been used as safe places of refuge, too.

While the inner resource can be helpful, having a real bundle of fur beside you can be priceless. For instance, pets can create a healing space for you when you are feeling loss. Oreo, my sister's Havenese was good at creating a healing space.

Cats for Comfort

Let's look for a change at cats and how they can assist in our healing. I have heard beautiful stories about cats and their ability to bring comfort and healing. Fluffy was the nursing home cat where Michelle worked as a nurse's aid. Michelle had a severe allergic reaction to cats, but not to Fluffy. It was unbelievable how Michelle described the fact that she could feel Fluffy in the break room without having any symptoms. Fluffy had a gift, a special role to play at the nursing home. Whenever it was getting close to the time for a resident to pass over and go home Fluffy would go into the room. She would cuddle up just before the patient passed and be with them until they died. She had that sixth sense and instinct that animals have around death. She would not leave their side and was there until they crossed over to the other side.

But things don't always go so smoothly. They can quickly turn into one of what I call "my pet peeves." I once (note the word "once") went to a therapist who had a cat with her in her consulting room. It was fine that she had a cat, she just omitted mentioning it when I called to make the appointment. Upon arrival, I had the awkward moment of not only her but her cat greeting me at the door where the therapist explained that the cat wouldn't be in the way, blah, blah, and blah. I have a history of cat allergies. My dog allergy is milder. I didn't have a great feeling standing at her door, but since I was there, I thought I'd give it a try. Let's just say this therapist wasn't a good fit and the cat at the doorway was my first clue. The cat therapist obviously didn't disclose this part of her therapy soon enough to prospective clients. This cat therapy experience was not a good one, so I can't say I was sold on cat therapy after this event.

Luckily, I had another healing experience once as well, when I went for a weeklong workshop about flower essences. Patrice, one of the owners of the flower farm and our teacher, told the story about how they were not planning on getting a cat when they started their flower farm. However, she had a dream about a white cat walking up their driveway one evening, and a few days later, Lily showed up. She was clearly there to stay. She was the most gorgeous soft, white cat ever! I haven't been around many cats, so I don't have much to compare to, but she was all things feminine.

Patrice told us Lily was a very independent cat and didn't particularly hang out with people much. We had some cat owners and lovers in the class who were all over her and she pretty much ignored them. One warm, sunny,

relaxed day in class, as many of us sat on the floor, in strutted Ms. Lily. She made a beeline to my lap and sat down to my and everyone else's amazement. A few weeks before, I was feeling pretty sad about the end of what I had thought was quite possibly the love of my life. Lily must have sensed I needed some "work," because I didn't flinch when she came to sit, but welcomed her. When she was

Lily, the healing cat

done, she just marched right out of the room without a glance to the right or the left. After she left, I felt much freer, lighter, and at peace. And I wasn't sniffing and sneezing like I had years ago when I was around cats in general. Had I outgrown my cat allergy? Or was I just not allergic to Lily?

I was fortunate to be staying in the guest house on the property during the workshop and spent many a moment lying on my stomach in the gardens, listening to music, soaking up the sun. Lily would find me and sit beside me. She wasn't done with me yet, and I felt like she helped me heal the loss in my heart. She was a special cat for sure; I never met another one like her. And she taught me about the healing power of cat lap time when I thought this was something only dogs were good at! What a gift that week was at the flower farm.

Therapy Dogs

Animal-assisted therapy can really help someone through some rough times as Lily taught me. I've been in sessions where the dog was an integral part of the trans-formation, too. I had, for instance, a massage therapist whose dog would hang out under the table and I found it comforting. He was a serious work dog, and the therapist said Madison couldn't wait to go to work in the morning.

I've had colleagues and friends who are healers who work with their dogs in their spaces, officially and unoffi-cially. Some therapists' protective companion dogs allow them to work with a greater population of clients. There actually is a certification program for dogs to become "therapy dogs." Then they can easily be admitted into hospitals and other public arenas, but I've known plenty of dogs that go into nursing homes and share the love without needing an official piece of paper.

A growing number of psychotherapists are using ther-apy animals to facilitate treatment, especially of children with emotional, social, and even physical problems. Along with other benefits, animals have been demon-strated to improve human cardiovascular health, reduce stress, decrease loneliness and depression, and facilitate social interactions. While Mitzie was quite the people dog, I think she wouldn't have been the greatest choice for such therapy. She liked to veg out and relax a lot. She took lots of sunbaths in the garden outside in the summer and napped in front of the heater vents in the winter. Like any good Taurus, she knew the higher side of the word, lazy and indulged in it often.

Max, the German Shepherd I knew, who worked as a therapy dog, liked children and helped many balance disturbances attributed to Attention Deficit Hyperactivity Disorder. His presence worked towards developing better self-regulation, self-esteem, and social behavior. A young woman who was in an abusive relationship found that

Max's protective presence in her therapy sessions helped give her the courage and fortitude to stand up for herself.

Dogs do embody unconditional positive regard and can really break the ice. I loved the idea of a therapy dog and believed it could help, but was still not sure it would be right for my practice. I thought the idea a bit tricky, as I wanted my client to feel one-hundred-percent comfortable and at ease and to keep distractions to a minimum. So while a dog could be a comfort, it could also be a distraction if it wasn't mature enough to quietly sit in the corner. However, I did love the idea of a dog being there to welcome clients and act as a grounding force during sessions.

I've always wondered if the use of a dog as a therapy dog really would be up to the comfort level of the clients. They might hesitate to tell me that they are not comfortable. Maybe if they like the dog, it would come to greet them at the door and then go off on its way. But even if the dog would be sitting quietly in a corner on its bed, I would ask myself if his presence would serve the client's highest and finest good.

Certified pet therapy dog

Dr. Fine, whose extensive, successful use of therapy animals in treating children is documented in *The Handbook on Animal-Assisted Therapy*, emphasized the challenges of working with these animals. He described one study in which the patient, a young boy with autism was helped by animal therapy. When the child was with the therapy dog, his levels of the stress hormone cortisol dropped; the levels rose again when the dog was taken away and dropped again when the dog was returned.

Fine also said, "You can't bring in just any animal to a therapy setting. The animal has to be very well-trained, reliable, and obedient and have the right temperament. It can't be overly anxious or easily startled. And the therapist has to know how to use it as a therapy adjunct, in combination with good psychotherapy. The animal is there to help support what the therapist is doing, to act as a catalyst and not a distraction. And, of course, animal-assisted interventions have to be safe for everyone involved—the patient *and* the animal."

One of my experiences of blending dogs and therapy, though, didn't sit so well with me. It happened when I went to do a Reiki trade with a new acquaintance at her home. She told me she had a dog and that I may see him upon arrival. She asked if I would wait for her before entering the gate to her house because she didn't want him to run out. As a dog lover, I thought nothing of it. I knew it was a bad sign when I pulled my car up to the driveway and saw a really tall fence and heard a loud, aggressive barking coming from behind it. The massage therapist came out tightly holding the dog by his collar and dragging him into the house. She invited me in. The dog quieted down once we were inside, and I made my greetings but my pulse was still racing from our first encounter.

Shortly after taking my first sip of tea, the dog suddenly and excitedly jumped up, placing his paws on me. Normally, this would not have been a big deal, but his claw had seared through my shirt to my skin. Ouch!

I thought it was an accident, but when I lifted my shirt, gasping at the sight of the marks and blood running down my side, I was concerned. The therapist didn't apologize and sided with her dog, saying, "He usually doesn't get so excited and act like this." *Maybe not, I thought, but he just punctured skin and you aren't exactly jumping up to offer a Band-Aid and you aren't taking responsibility for your dog.* I felt she was somehow blaming me for her dog's behavior. I survived, but that connection obviously never went further.

You might understand I still had my doubts, but seeing a therapy dog in action at the Red Cross shelter after a school shooting in Portland where I volunteered as a Disaster Mental Health counselor, changed all that. I met not one but three therapy dogs that day in Portland. All were hypo-allergic beauties who worked hard despite the heat to make sure anyone who needed some attention that day got it. They just know intuitively who to turn to. While the kids and parents stood in the beating hot sun for hours the afternoon of the shooting, waiting to get their belongings, therapy dogs were there to soothe the shocking effects from the morning trauma. It was a most convincing argument. Dogs are really master therapists.

Pet Transference: Dogs as Security Objects

Most of us feel sometimes the need to return to our past to clear up old emotional business. In the process, we often use new persons or objects to redirect the feelings and desires we find in our past towards the present. It can happen often, for instance when we are around children. We often transfer to children not just all the values we have, but all of the traumas we have, too. We see in a child what is really about cherishing good times or we see unfinished business from not-so-good times. For example, let's say my neighbor girl is eleven when her dog dies. I might unconsciously transfer my feelings about pets that have passed over onto the neighbor girl because I was around the same age when Mitzie died.

Transference is not restricted to people. We attempt to find peace, resolution, closure, too, through pets old and new for what is still unfinished business. So dogs are objects of transference as well. I've told you, Boston Terriers were in my family the animals that brought comfort and reassurance. First my mother had for a short time one, Mickey, after facing the loss of her father—at an early, then I connected our Mitzie with warm feelings of childhood, love, and nurturance. Although, I connected my mother's home-baked chocolate-chip cookies with comfort food as well! Later, I have transferred a lot of the nostalgic feelings I have from my youth onto dogs, including stuffed ones. I still have a stuffed animal dog from my childhood stored away in a box somewhere. "Spot" was there for me as a safety crutch. The stuffed animal has acquired many extra mystery spots from being dragged around that weren't part of Spot's original design. And his ears are pretty ragged.

Dogs, alive, dead or stuffed, can be counted on for comfort in painful times, but if, as an adult, I'm still calling upon the stuffed animal as a kind of substitute connection, there is a problem. Spot needs to be seen as an old transitional object of comfort that served me well but is from a past long gone. It had a beautiful meaning that brought back memories of being a child. It's no longer the same as when I was young. Still, my Spot remained in the attic for a while as a dear possession, because of his ability to be a source of comfort and reassurance as a child.

Vintage Brindle Bostons

Transference just happens. It's not like you can suddenly just decide to avoid it altogether. Maybe I have some unfinished business I still transfer over to pets. Or, in addition, perhaps I still cling to things like jewelry, letters, photos, and mementos too tightly. It is not necessarily a sign of weakness, but recognition, that things hold meanings, and, like our dog did, can help us through difficult times. Like objects, pets can help us reconcile people, places, and events from our pasts.

When I look at the objects in my possession, I like to

look at them as if they still hold the magic and mystery of the past—almost like they are sacred objects—and when I am done with having them, I release them and let them go. Knick knacks, artwork, furniture, travel souvenirs, favorite sweaters mostly outgrow their welcome and end up in the Goodwill bin eventually. Have we used the possession in the past year? Is there a way we can take a Polaroid of it instead of holding onto it? A photo-taking hobby has led to a few boxes of photo albums and CDs of photos that soon need to be digitalized, as they will disintegrate, too. Maybe I'll just have to let them turn to dust. If we try to hold on too tight and control everything we may just want to avoid grief.

In David Richo's book, *When the Past Becomes the Present,* his subtitle "Persons, Pets, Places, and Things" talks about how we use pets to establish a sense of stability. When I read his book he was a great inspiration for me and I am happy to let him come back in my writing. A pet is a security object. It can be used to comfort us and maintain connection just like any other person, place, or thing. For instance, dogs love unconditionally, they are loyal, cheerful, and dependable. There is a cute saying about how a dog slowly winds its way not only into your house and heart but into your bed. Sometimes it sleeps on more of your pillow than you do! Dogs can often be seen as persons and are treated like children or as partners. Dogs can even get better treatment than people give themselves—or other family members—for that matter. Concern about a dog or pet's health and safety becomes paramount. This deep bond of attachment can become important to our happiness. This can all be quite healthy, but there comes a time when it is useful to be aware of the part that transference is playing.

How much of human need is being fulfilled by an animal? Is a sense of loneliness being filled up by Fido's faithful presence after a break up, a bad day, or the death of a loved one? Care needs to be taken that dogs do not become all-encompassing substitutes for human connection.

How does one balance pet versus human connection? A pet seems to fill a void that is there. In my mother's case it was missing her father who had recently died. Other instances when a pet fills an empty space are missing a partner who has died, not having a partner or the love of a parent or sibling. A dog is a handful, a responsibility to feed. And exercising it and getting it fresh air all take time away from social contacts. If one has a full life, a pet makes it even fuller. If one has relational gaps, a pet can fill that empty space, but it begs the question of whether that happens in addition or in lieu of filling that gap with human connections.

Pamela's mother had recently lost her husband with whom she did everything. He also handled all the affairs of the home and she felt totally lost, stricken and useless without him. She got a dog, Camilla, who quickly took front and center of her life. The dog came before all else, at the expense of making time to connect with her children. For example, when they would be over having dinner and the dog would come into the room, Pamela's mother would become fixated on the dog to the point of annoying Pamela and the rest of the family. What's a healthy relationship with a pet? Pets are animals and owners are humans. If we habitually ignore the people in the room and focus on the pet, is that out of balance? In this case, Camilla is helping Pamela's mother recover from the loss of her husband. He is filling an emptiness as she grieves for her husband. But what do you think, should she leave out her kids?

How do you know when the balance tilts too far toward animal over human connection? Perhaps you have known someone who leaned a little too much on a pet for connection versus fostering human interactions. In these circumstances, the pet even might be treated too much like a person rather than the animal it really is. When I was single I came close to getting a dog once and, looking back, am glad I didn't. I was working long hours and traveling a bit. If I would have had to run home to take out a dog, would I have been out dating as much? Turns out the traveling bit was key for me because that is how I eventually met my husband. I think there are great pet-sitting options for pet owners. But back then if I had a pet to worry about I may not have taken a vacation to Europe that summer.

Nonetheless, I'm still sentimental about Christmas and birthdays and carry around plenty of light celebratory spirit in my subconscious from these remainders of the past, but there is some heavy Samsonite baggage left behind there, as well. In a way, expectations, fulfilments and disappointments are buried together for good or ill underneath the Christmas tree. Every year, I get a chance to bring bits and pieces out into the light to be freed and, in doing so, what remains over time, are the joyous feelings in the present. Inevitably, that joy is connected to the nostalgic past. Hence, our family's Boston Terrier ornament-giving ritual.

We have still have Mitzie's stocking in the family. The letters of her name have long since started to fall off as the glue dissolves. I imagine that I can still remember gluing the little pieces of wrapping ribbon to name her stocking. She would get a bone and some doggie treats. We didn't have a fireplace, so the stockings were on the hinges of our front door. Her stocking was always hung the lowest so that she could get to it easily. She didn't know it was Christmas and we never celebrated her Taurus birthday. But she was there every Christmas through my early childhood, along with all the anticipation, music, candies, presents, and bows; hence, she became part of the transference of what holidays mean for us as a family. No wonder she is still alive in our hearts and shows up in a box under the tree or hanging from a Christmas tree in some form or other.

A dog's loyalty can make us feel grounded and secure in our present lives; dogs typically stick close by and are always there for us. That is, until they depart from this earth. Richo suggests, "Transference can then be a reminder of how much we missed in our past. A dog is also a reminder of how much we have to be thankful for in pets who so reliably and willingly make up for our woeful losses."[2]

The bond to a pet can become very strong. On a logical level, we know they are not like us, they belong to a different kingdom, the animal kingdom. Emotionally, though, dogs in transference can become like family members. There is no separation when we yield portions from our psyche onto a pet. Depending on how much we surrendered to the transference, we may see little to no difference between how others treat us and how they treat our pets.

Pet owners can be so close to their pets that they take any slights to or criticisms of their pets as personal insults or rejection. Owners can have difficulty separating their own emotions from what others think about their pet. I've seen this myself, for instance. A friend's puppy unintentionally broke some skin biting me while playing. Months later over coffee my friend told me her puppy had bitten not only her a few times but another family member, too. Only then, I mentioned getting nipped myself that day playing with her puppy at her house, which I thought she was aware of. Her eyes welled up with tears and her feelings got hurt that I had not told her sooner. I tried to console her and said, "I thought you knew and it wasn't that big of a deal. I'm Ok, we're Ok."

To make it more complicated, my friend was struggling with a health condition of her puppy. It would probably need surgery and might have to be put down. My friend was asking me what I thought she should do. A listening ear is what she really needed in that moment. And then I learned a lesson the hard way. I told her a story I had just heard that week that later I wished I had kept to myself. It was about someone who knew a woman had been bitten by the same breed dog as hers and it wasn't a happy ending. The victim forced the owners to put the dog down, a terrible story, no doubt. The wrong story and the wrong moment. So the story struck an unexpected chord. My friend abruptly left the coffee-house and didn't return my email or call for weeks. Although it may be more complicated, these silences were the beginning to the end of our friendship. I'm still sad about losing that friendship. Just like other deaths, the loss of a friendship is hard. I learned many lessons that day, but the one that stands out is that sometimes it's better to say nothing at all, than attempt to console a distraught pet owner.

Dogs also say something about what we learned or were never taught about boundaries. The electric underground dog fences we have in our neighborhood encourage the dogs to honor the boundaries created by their owners. Is a barking dog sometimes merely reacting to the stimulus of someone walking by their home? Or are they distressed and expressing suppressed loneliness, boredom or anger? If a dog barks fiercely at people walking by, how is the pet corrected? Or is it accepted that no dog is perfect? Training them not to be fierce or display agitation may, for example, bring up whether anger was under- or over-expressed in our upbringing. Harriet Lerner in her book, *Dance of Anger*, suggests that anger is often underexpressed by women. I would have to agree that that was the case for me and my upbringing.

Transference affects us at all ages and stages of life.

How we treat our dogs may say something about unfinished emotions from the past. As a child, I used to pull our dog's tail, and because she was a Boston Terrier, it was a nearly nonexistent tail. How cruel I was to the poor dog. Perhaps I was transferring some unexpressed resentment onto our dog. I've learned pretty quickly, thanks to Mitzie, that isn't the way to go. Dogs can teach you how to love and also how to channel your anger into healthy outlets. Walking Mitzie was a great way to let off extra steam. Exercise has always been a great way to release any unfinished anger business. Am I trying to recapture moments from my childhood pets and heal through transference onto them unfinished business with other people? Sure I am. Remember transference just happens. The trick is to pay attention to naming the transference, which frees us to live more in the present while honoring our past.

Maybe it is time to have a closer look at those transferences that present us with unfinished business and therefore with opportunities to move on.

Part II

DEATH

In Between Pets

Boston looking down from heaven

"If there are no dogs in Heaven, then when I die I want to go where they went."

—Will Rogers

"You think dogs will not be in heaven? I tell you, they will be there long before any of us."

—Robert Louis Stevenson

"Heaven goes by favor. If it went by merit, you would stay out and your dog would go in."

—Mark Twain

L ife gives us opportunities for joy in abundance, but, in the end, all that is given can be taken away. Life is a mixture of sunshine and shadow. Grief is part of living.

I hope you have fully enjoyed the stories and teachings of the pets in my life, but now I must turn to the shadow. Nearly all of the pets I have brought on stage are no longer with me in real life, but they came back to me in the reality of my inner world and from there I could almost feel them. Of course, it all started with our family dog, Mitzie, my first dog that I introduced to you already. In between my own fun memories and under all the continuing family rituals, I felt my grief growing and I found I had work to do. Even in death, my dogs served me as master-teachers in letting me face the unfinished business of my grief. Just like in therapy, dreams played in this process a leading role.

I have seen it often happening with clients when I listen to their stories of pet loss. Grieving a pet lets them face inner realities about coming to terms with death, our loved ones and our own. It was the same for me. The memories of my first dog made me, for instance, face the unfulfilled needs of my inner child that was devastated by a loss that seemed to have little meaning or explanation. Where did my pet go? So my writing turned from a celebration of life into a "grief memoir," as it were, just another healing power of the presence of pets in my life.

I share my musings and dreams and those of my clients to take a closer look at grief and to explore it, not merely as something to get over with, but as a slow, delicate process of allowing my love to take on this task and transform my grief into a lighter form. In this way and after many years, my beloved pet companions have brought me comfort and closure.

Unfinished Mourning

Why write so much about a childhood pet? Because there is grief within lying dormant that never fully worked its way through the body and soul. Death and dying aren't easy subjects to talk about. My great-grandparents were immigrants and seasoned by hardships. They were farmers who brought lessons of life and death to me. They were no strangers to loss. I wish I had had a book when I was a little girl that talked about how to deal with death and dying of loved ones and pets. When we first started to see those gray hairs on our dog it was a shock. Even though we knew their lifespan is so much shorter than the years we humans enjoy, we never wanted to admit our dog was getting old. When Mitzie started to gray and slow down it felt as if it happened overnight.

Mitzie in old age

A cloud hung over our house for more than a year. There were brushes with death. Grandparents on either side of my family and our beloved pet were aging quickly. The first was my father's mother. She was in the hospital for months before she passed away on a bitter cold day in January. Ten days later, my mother's stepfather crossed over, too. And a year or so later, Mitzie died. At the same time, my close friend Valerie was getting weaker from her leukemia. We couldn't play together any more.

What were our family's reactions to or participation in grief? Losses within the family required mutually visible grief. For instance, when a family member dies, it is not enough to grieve by ourselves. It has to be a family affair and grief doesn't come easily, especially when we are young. I don't remember seeing either of my parents openly grieve that year. As you know, my mother's father passed away early in her life and Mickey my mother's aunt's dog, was there to comfort her and her siblings. Mickey died just a year after he arrived in town to stay with my mother's family. He got a cancer tumor on his stomach that grew to be the size of a tennis ball so he went back to Aunt Gracie's house to die at home. My mother doesn't remember saying goodbye or crying over Mickey and doesn't know if he was buried or cremated.

In these modern times, it's more recognized that we need to see our parents crying so we can mirror one another's grief. Grief wasn't always so easy to talk about during my childhood and that wasn't uncommon. So our ability to grieve was stunted around our family dog. I remember my parents checked in with us about how we were holding up after the loss. In some ways, grief was inconsolable for us because we didn't have a context to grieve together. We didn't bury Mitzie in the backyard or do a memorial that would have brought some closure to our loss together as a family.

We may be inquiring about each other's grief now through immortalizing the dog in Mitzie gifts, for instance. Richo states, "Any feeling reaction of great magnitude may be a condensed set of experiences that get bunched over the years into one theme."[3]

For instance, the three deaths of a grandfather, grandmother, and family dog may have left some unfinished mourning that got encircled into this collection of Boston mementos found in our homes.

Writing my Boston story has been a bit like going through some form of a grief repetition compulsion—psychobabble for a psychological phenomenon in which a person repeats a traumatic circumstance over and over again. Repetition compulsion includes re-enacting the event or putting oneself in situations where the event is likely to happen again. This reliving can take the form of dreams in which memories and feelings of what happened are repeated.

Why put myself through the grief again?

Perhaps I never grieved fully the first time. In the process of writing this book, I shed many tears and smiled over many fond memories. The more I wrote, the more I let go of the loss of our dear Boston Terrier and the more I took back a part of my inner child. I saw where the past is the present through the eyes of our dog. Our pets are like family members, and sometimes it takes years, even decades, for people to let go of them. I've seen grief manifest in so many ways in myself and others. Pets become enshrined in our hearts. My husband tells that when his sister's poodle, Pedro, died, his mother and sister cried for weeks about the loss of their poodle. Around this same time his maternal grandmother died. Perhaps their tears were mixed, too.

I'm a sentimental person. My room was a shrine after I left for high school. I had a friend from college visit one weekend and he remarked how strange it felt to him that my room seemed as if I had never left. I still had all my trinkets, ribbons, books, and bows around. I started boxing them up shortly after. Of course, some of it went to the attic for me to go through once again many years later. While my family and I are not hoarders, we do like to store mementos from the past. Perhaps that is why we enshrine our pet as well. I am grateful that the family hung on to some of those keepsakes. They helped bring closure to the loss of Mitzie decades later.

Hard Losses

One of my favorite animal movies is *My Dog Skip*. The final scene is a heartbreaker and goes something like this: "I received a trans-Atlantic call one day from my daddy telling me Skip had died. He and my mama wrapped him in my baseball jacket. They buried him out under the elm tree, they said. That wasn't totally true. For he really lay buried in my heart." Dogs do forever remain deep in our hearts.

Mitzie and part-time pets I've been lucky enough to have on loan have taught me much about grief. Master therapists in the form of a pet, help people grieve every day, whether it is a loss like a child grow-ing up and mov-ing out of the house, a divorce or a more final passing, like the loss of a family member. Or perhaps it's a chronic ill-ness that limits one's day-to-day life in some way. Pets and the pet-centered approach help pave the way to healing. The journey of grief is unique for all but there are some common factors.

It's always hard to lose a pet, particularly when it has to be put down. The challenge of pet loss is made more difficult when having to decide whether to euthanize an aged or suffering pet. Grief is a delicate thing and each pet owner goes through it differently. Just to know that there is a beginning, middle and end can be a source of com-fort. Unfortunately, that doesn't mean you can skip going through the pain of grief. It is like a portal that feels like it will never end, but grief will transform nonetheless. The average is a year to get over the death of a significant loved one. Grief that goes beyond that, as in my case, just means that there are some other factors at play having to do with some unfinished business in my inner world. Then it isn't so much about the pet as it about going deeper within to see where the past has become the present. What within myself needs to be grieved, let go of so that I can be fully in the present, feeling pleasure, gratitude and joy in the here and now.

Sometimes you don't lose the pet to death, but for oth-er obvious reasons. I had a client whose pet began biting others shortly after they brought home their newborn baby. The family's heart was broken because they had to give their dog away; they couldn't risk it being jealous and harming the baby.

Our family nearly had to get rid of Mitzie when the results from my allergy tests came back stating I was allergic to some degree to dogs. I do remember driving home from the allergist feeling scared, worried about Mitzie and thinking, *I hope something bad isn't going to happen to her now.* It wasn't a surprise that cats made me sneeze and wheeze, but I had never felt any symptoms around dogs.

My allergist told my mother that they should get rid of the dog. My mother remembers telling both me and my sister separately. We burst into tears immediately upon hearing her say, "We are going to have to do something about Mitzie." We were devastated and couldn't imagine life without her.

In the end, she was blocked from the bedroom hallway with a cardboard box and allowed to stay. I can't imagine what that would have been like if they would have had to give her away because of my allergies. That would have been like a premature death. It would have broken not only my heart, but my family's. Mitzie was already eleven years old when this all happened, and maybe it was preparing us for what was yet to come, her departure from this earth.

Psychic Pet Dreams

When my roommate moved out, I was sad to see her go and really missed both her and her pet parakeet Oscar. She left Oscar with me for a few days of pet therapy while she was getting settled in. He helped ease the loss in my transition of living again solo. When she came back to get him and we said our goodbyes, I cried, mostly because I would miss her but didn't realize yet how much I would miss her little yellow bird. Oscar was gone, but little did I know how strong the connection was and that it would live on.

A year or more passed since my roommate and Oscar moved out-of-state. One night, I had a startling and vivid dream about Oscar that left me in a cold sweat. In the dream, Oscar was frantic, parched, and opening and closing his beak. He wasn't singing like his usual cheerful self. He screeched at me that he was thirsty and needed water. I told myself, *It's just a dream, I will call my friend in the morning*, and drifted back to sleep.

The next morning, I spoke with my friend and briefly mentioned the dream about Oscar crying out for water. We ended our call, and, a few hours later, I got the devastating news from her telling me Oscar was dead. She had checked in on him and found he didn't have any water in his dish. The heat of the sun had evaporated it and the dish was bone dry.

That is what you could call a pre-cognitive dream, or what I call a psychic pet dream, and they happen to people all the time. All I knew is that Oscar had reached out to me for help and I hadn't reacted. It took some time to forgive myself and move on.

I went to a weekend of seminars at Omega Institute in the early 1990s where three speakers, a psychotherapist, an intuitive and a master hypnotherapist, all spoke about death, dying, and contacting heaven and the other side. A woman at the end of one of the sessions got up and asked the hypnotherapist about a series of dreams she had where a family member had died prematurely. Months later, when the family member died in real life, she wanted to know why she was the only one in the family to have had dreams about this upcoming death. The speaker turned around the question and she ended up answering it for herself. She responded that maybe it was because she was the one who either needed that extra bit of time to get used to the idea of losing the family member before it happened or maybe it was because she was a healer and could help others grieve the loss, having had a bit of a head start. Or maybe she was particularly close to this family member and could help ease the passing. There was a reason for it, that was for sure, and maybe nobody really knows how the heavens prepare us for loss.

The year that Oscar died was the same year I lost my dear friend Bob to AIDS. He was the first person or pet to whom I was close who had died since my pre-teen years when my grandparents, Mitzie, my close friend Valerie and my classmate Mark passed over. My first encounter with losing someone close came when Valerie was diagnosed with leukemia in fifth grade. In every one of my childhood birthday party pictures I see her until she got sick. Valerie was a kindred spirit with bright red hair and a vivid imagination. She slowly faded away until she died at the age of thirteen. My sixth grade classmate Mark was hit by a drunk driver and killed that following year. We went as a class to his memorial. Mark's Italian grandmother actually babysat my sister and I on occasion when my parents went out of town and made the best spaghetti. My sixth grade teacher, Mr. Mulberry led a discussion upon our return from the memorial and did a good job letting us know it was OK to cry and feel sad. He encouraged us to talk about our feelings. I don't think any of us talked much, but I remember being comforted by his sharing so openly about the process of death and dying.

Unfinished mourning from my "inner child" was channeled through the deaths of Bob and Oscar. My belief in the soul and afterlife in not just humans but animals too became stronger after these experiences with death and dying. Some part of me knew that what we called death was merely a transition. And in the following years, dogs continued to demonstrate how to die with dignity.

Goodbye to Brewster

Edgar Cayce, the famous healer from Virginia, suggests that we have limitless guidance and counsel readily available to us in our dreams. He suggests that precognitive guidance occurs in dreams because, by being forewarned, the dreamer is better able to respond to the situation. The dream attunes an individual to this storehouse of experience that has been set in motion.[4]

Five months before our beloved part-time dog Brewster was put down, I had a dream. Even though he wasn't my dog he found a way to weave his way not only into my heart but also into my unconscious.

> *Brewster has slipped on his butt and walks sideways down a dirt path that is very slippery. I am with him; my husband is in the house. After Brewster slips, he falls off to the right of the slope and crawls into a hole. I wonder how I can help him get back up on the path. He is heavy and scared. I call my husband, not expecting him to help since he is angry that Brewster had gone to the bathroom in our yard (something he rarely did in real life), but my husband appears right away. Brewster's legs have failed him; it's too hard for him.*

I woke up, knowing we would be traveling for a while and wondered if he would be gone by the time we would get home from vacation. I decided I would move the soccer toy away from his spare bed in our garage because I sensed he wouldn't need it anymore. But luckily we were back in time to say goodbye.

Like many German Shepherds, Brewster had arthritic hips in his old age and he was on aspirin for the pain. We really spoiled Brewster before he was put down. We pampered him all week. He got lamb bones galore, walks to get the paper with us, massages on his arthritic body. I couldn't look at him that last day when I gave him his final bone. Afterwards, I had to get rid of the leftover dog treats. The UPS and FedEx men would miss Brewster too, I presumed. They would come to the neighbor's home with deliveries in one hand and a bone for Brewster in the other, but Brewster was gone and wouldn't be there to claim it.

The day we said goodbye I wrote this in my diary: "I'll forever hear his collar jingling outside. It's like a morgue here today, so quiet. I realize I'm glad we will be putting in a deck in the backyard so it will change the memories and scenery. Nice because we are less likely to be reminded of Brewster."

I told my mother that Brewster would be put down. She had probably said what I share next before but somehow it struck home more deeply because of Brewster. It was amazing to me. She said she was so sorry she didn't bring Mitzie home from the vet so we could say goodbye before she was put down. Mom had only learned that morning from the vet that he could give her some medicine, but that she wouldn't be comfortable. It would be best to put her down soon, he had said. Mom apologized again for not bringing Mitzie home before they put her to sleep. I said, "It's okay, Mom. You didn't want Mitzie to suffer any longer and I'm so glad she didn't, either." It felt really good that we talked about it. "You did the right thing not bringing her back home," I said. "It would have been too hard on Mitzie and she was suffering."

I told her I remembered clearly the morning she took Mitzie to the vet telling us to say goodbye because we might not see her again. I sat down next to Mitzie in her cubby hole. She lay in her orange tub looking up at me. I remember petting her and starting to cry, silently saying a goodbye. I walked to school, crying the whole way. I knew deep down it would be the last time I saw her. Earlier that week, Mitzie had gotten disoriented and ended up down the street at a neighbor's home. Often, kids know when their dog is nearing death. She had been on heart pills for a little while. Mitzie was suffering and coughed all night before Mom took her to the vet. He said she had congestive heart failure. So Mom made the wise decision to put her down. It was healing for Mom to talk about it that day with me. Mitzie died sometime in the spring. Our family's best guess is that it was in the month of April. Wouldn't that be interesting if we were actually able to order a death certificate for our pet just like we can for humans? I was eleven years old. Mitzie was nearly fourteen years old; pretty old in dog years. I remember crying at my desk; it was a sea of unbearable sadness.

Things seemed to come full circle with Brewster by being able to be around and say goodbye right up to the last hour. That was something I never got to do with Mitzie, be there until the end. Brewster met Mom and she liked to spoil him by feeding him bones, too. It felt full circle to have the sadness and grief around Mitzie acknowledged and validated because of Brewster's passing.

He came over the night before he was put down and sat while we grilled. I remember watching him eat his final evening snack of rack of lamb and thinking, *you can eat as much as you want Brewster because it won't matter tomorrow.* My husband and I had a hard time sleeping that night. We knew the vet was coming in the morning. That morning I walked to the edge separating our lawn from our neighbor's and stood with Brewster in the sun for the last time. I loved walking there with him.

Brewster

Later when we saw the vet's van pull up, we went into our meditation room and lit a candle for Brewster. Our next-door neighbors dearly loved their Brewster and were so kind to indulge and share him with us. We wanted to set an intention for a peaceful passing for him. That meant that I wasn't going to lose it until after he had crossed over. I figured it would be easier for him if we remembered the good times together.

And then it was over. I'm still sad about losing him. I sobbed for a while in my husband's arms and we watched the vet van drive away. It brought memories of missing Mitzie after she died—no longer hearing the sound of her feet above me from our basement rec room or seeing her welcome me when I came home. I wouldn't hear Brewster's collar jingle anymore, or see him come around the corner of the yard. I wouldn't see him sit at our front door and watch down the driveway, alert to all the happenings in our yards. I wouldn't walk him and see him give me those puppy eyes as he eats.

He liked being petted. He was an active dog, something new for me, and I liked it. I couldn't wait to get up when we watched him, to see his loving face, his excitement about starting the day. He loved to sit at our front door. Knowing that he wasn't really allowed inside all the way, he would just sneak his front paws over the door stoop. It didn't matter that he let in cold air, we just liked having him at our doorstep.

Taking away Brewster's two water bowls was hard and I kept one for a year after his passing. Remember, he was a "rent-a-dog." So the dish was a plastic cereal bowl I grabbed on the fly and never imagined it would become a treasured memento and part of a pet loss packet, stored in the shed to be removed a year later. Later on I learned from Susan McElroy's book, *Why Buffalo Dance,* that it is called a spirit packet. Brewster was in our lives only for a short time but left a healing memory, part of which was stored away in a simple piece of plastic.

I went rollerblading that evening and saw more dogs on the path than ever before. In my imagination, they were all looking me straight in the eye as I sped past them.

Maltese on the Road

As my sister and I were driving one sunny morning, Maddie, as I called her, dashed out of nowhere onto the busy road. She was a little white Maltese, frantically darting in between the cars. When we first saw the little white ball of fur, we became concerned that she was bound to get hit in the rush of traffic. But she made it around the corner where we pulled over to the side of the road. My sister rushed out to see if she could coax Maddie to safety. Another man in front of us had the same idea.

Maddie was a good thirty feet away and nervously moving up the sidewalk as the busy traffic sped by. The plan was that I would get the leash and treats in the trunk and follow. As I shut the SUV hatch, Maddie seemed to become startled and darted into the road, where a speeding Ford Mustang, tires screeching, hit Maddie. I screamed and turned my head, as it was too much to view. We were too late. I felt helpless and a pang of guilt as I slammed the hatch, wondering if that really had startled her. I couldn't take away the pain she was feeling.

My sister was quickly by Maddie's side, gently taking her in her arms and moving to the median in between the traffic. My sister started cranial sacral physical therapy on Maddie whose breathing was shallow and her eyes were darting back and forth. She was scared and in shock. Her pelvis had been hit and there was blood trickling out of her little mouth. I had never sat beside a pet or loved one as they passed over before. It was overwhelming, but we didn't want the dog to be alone, so we kept vigil.

I sat with Maddie, holding her gaze and feeling the emotions of sensing another's pain. All I wanted to do was protect her and keep her from hearing the chaos and commotion around her. The man who hit her approached, flustered, angry, and full of excuses about how the dog shouldn't have been there and the car in front of him stopped too soon. A woman came close, arguing with him about driving too fast. In the corner of my eye, I saw a policeman approach, who luckily was a few cars behind the speeding Mustang. All the commotion was not helping Maddie and my sister wisely told the two it would be better if they took their argument elsewhere. Then it was only Maddie and her eyes that mattered. Everything else faded away.

In the meantime, Maddie had slipped into unconsciousness; her heart had gone from being shallow to stopping all together. Her eyes were closed. Would she return to life or move on? I placed my hand on her little chest with loving care, my sister encouraging me, thinking Reiki might comfort her. In that moment, her whole body jerked up into our hands and I suddenly felt the rhythmic rise of her chest as she starting breathing again. It was like time stopped. I was blown away. She opened her eyes and gazed at me with a look of fear and anxiety. I held her gaze, silently telling her what a good dog she was. I only wanted to ease her suffering and calm her fears. My sister spoke to her very softly and slowly using a soothing voice and I followed suit. We told her it was okay to go, that she was such a great dog and much loved, that she was such a good dog—so sweet, so loving. We gave her permission to die.

We were in a bubble, and it seemed that everything else around us had stopped. The policeman who had dealt with the two arguing kept all others who approached at a distance. My sister continued to treat Maddie and I left my hand on her body feeling her warmth. Her body had been traumatized and her soul was looking for release. I remember a woman crying about how she had seen the whole thing. But it was like the rest of the world was outside us and it was only the two of us with Maddie hoping she would recover but knowing all along she was dying.

We wanted her to reach the other side with as much peace, ease, and comfort as possible. Time passed. Her breathing was not getting smoother, but more faint and more labored. And then Maddie breathing stopped altogether. Suddenly she was so still. She felt warm. Every nerve inside me was electric with a light that seemed to hover over the median.

No one who sits with the dying ever remains untouched. It was a kind of holy experience. It was an honor. And I knew that dying was much more than the process of her little ball of fur body shutting down; it was a letting go, spiritually and emotionally. The paradox—or more like a gift—was that I got to honor Maddie's passing in a different way than I got to honor Mitzie's. As we walked away, I imagined all the dogs I knew on the other side; Brewster, Brigitte, Jazz, and Mitzie were there to greet Maddie. I said a prayer that she would find peace and joy and that her owners would be located and find some closure.

I like to think Maddie had a happy life. In my fantasy, Maddie lived with the Johnson family, with little Dick and Jane, on 42nd Street in a small subdivision of Anywhere, USA. Maddie was a smart little dog who loved to cuddle up and snuggle in Jane's lap at night. When they came home from school, Maddie would be there to shower them with kisses and run and play in the yard. She was so smart that she didn't need a leash—or so her owners thought. One sunny day, Maddie saw one of her dog friends across the street and ran over to play. They quickly became distracted by another dog, Spot, racing down the street. Maddie followed Spot until she ran so far she didn't know her way home. Frantic, she raced through the streets.

We stayed with Maddie until animal rescue came to take her away. They were there in a matter of minutes. A dog lover himself, the policeman followed us back to our car. Surprisingly, he soon had us in stitches telling us stories about his little dog waiting for him at home. They had a routine where she would crawl up on his lap in the Lazy Boy chair and take a long nap with him. Imagine this burly, tough cop cuddling up with his fluffy dog after a hard day's work. She helped him take away the stress.

Feeling little Maddie's body respond to my touch reminded me that we all have the healing power of touch in our hands, and that it can be activated through emotion. The movie, *Powder* provides a glimpse of that healing power. In the movie, Jeremy Reed, whose nickname is Powder, is a young man who can sense the thoughts of the people around him. His brain possesses a powerful electromagnetic charge, which causes electrical objects to function abnormally when he is around them as well as when he becomes emotional.

On a hunting trip, Harley, a deputy who is hunting with the boys, has shot a doe, which is now dying. Anguished by the animal's death, Powder touches both the deer and Harley so that he will feel the pain the deer he has killed is feeling. He is inducing in Harley what some assume is a seizure. Harley, however, admits to Doug that Powder had actually caused him to feel the pain and fear of the dying deer and he cannot bring himself to take another life. Because of the experience, Harley removes all of his guns from his house. Powder is a great example of the power of touch and how we are all interconnected.

What did it mean that a little white Maltese that looked just like my friend Jenny's dog had crossed my path? Or that she reminded us a bit of Oreo? My sister knew what it meant for her. Oreo would be gone within a month of our encounter with Maddie. Perhaps Maddie was sent to help prepare the way for grieving Oreo.

A year later, Jenny's Coco, passed, too, and I was there to say goodbye when she was put down. All of these experiences with dogs and death: Brewster, Maddie, Oreo and Coco helped me with my unfinished grieving over not just Mitzie but with that sea of sadness, as my husband calls it, that we all carry inside. Maybe because of these experiences, I will have a tad more empathy when I sit with others going through grief. Maybe it was about opening my heart and just being there in the moment. Because of dogs, I personally have become more familiar with the death and dying process. Because of Maddie, I retrieved another lost piece of my inner child that was silently grieving Mitzie in the place of unfinished mourning.

More Passings

Dogs can make up the heart and soul of a family. People can grieve when a pet dies as if a child has passed away. I was lucky I was around to say goodbye to Oreo before he was put down. The poor guy could barely walk, so we pushed him around in a doggy stroller. It was so funny to see this gray-haired dog being wheeled everywhere like he was a puppy again. But that is what the end of life does to us; it brings us right back to where we started, fresh and vulnerable as a newborn puppy. I took him for walks in the park and set him down so he could smell the fresh grass and air. What amazed me was that no matter how much pain he was in, he was always wagging his tail in the morning and smiling to greet me and the day. He seemed to know death was coming and had a quiet dignity and courage in his final weeks. Did his brother Dash know how sick he was and what was ahead?

Dash's windblown look

I flew back home just two weeks before Oreo died. In the weeks that followed, I kept getting a picture in my mind's eye of his brother, Dash. I sensed along with others that he was deeply troubled and depressed over the loss of his sibling.

Family members reported that the only joys in his life were getting out of the house and riding in the car with the windows down. Hearing about Dash's difficulties acted as a mirror to help the family together grieve and cope with Oreo's passing, so I mailed a flower-essence remedy to Dash, which made me feel better. Much of grief is not personal; it is transpersonal, collective. We are each part of the web of life. There is a mountain of grief in the world we all tap into when we grieve for a pet.

I was honored to be able to be with my friend when she put down her dear Maltese, Coco. Coco gave me love and lap hugs when I really needed them after a hard breakup and I feel honored Jenny allowed me to be there during Coco's peaceful passing. How amazing was it that she got to go in the comfort of her home . . . priceless. Coco taught me a lot about the power of giving and receiving. I wanted to be there because I had been on the receiving end of Coco's love and felt like I got to give back a glimmer of that by being at her passing.

After she got the lethal shot, Coco had the most calm, serene, puppy-dog look as she lay on Jenny's shoulder . . . the most peaceful passing a dog could hope for at home with all her creature comforts and a web of viral and heavenly love surrounding her. Angel wings hovered over her house that day! I heard ringing in my ear maybe a minute before she gasped her last breath. Must have been one of her light angels, I believe. It was just like in the Jimmy Stewart movie, *It's a Wonderful Life*, when angel Clarence gets his wings and the bell rings! Jenny was so comforting and calm, holding her Coco and being with her during her passing, telling her what a good dog she was, giving her permission to go.

It was so healing to be there at Coco's passing. It reminded me again of my mother talking about how she felt bad that we didn't get to say goodbye to Mitzie. True, I didn't go to the vet that day; I was in school. I never really felt, though, that I missed out. Regardless, I feel more at peace having been there with Coco and imagining for a moment that this is how it could have been with our family dog if the vet van had come to our home. Later that day, I went rollerblading at the park. It seemed I had come full circle because I spotted so many Boston Terrier dogs at the park that day, which of course made me think of Mitzie. I felt a new found sense of peace in my heart around Mitzie mingled with feelings of sorrow for Jenny's loss of Coco.

The Cycle of Life

Sometimes I feel like I'm living a scene from the 1970s *Wild Kingdom* television show, living on a few acres surrounded by woods. We have had up-close and personal encounters with bunnies, birds, frogs, cats, coyotes, bears, deer and raccoons. I have had a natural lesson in letting animals find their own way rather than believing they need to be rescued. Therapists take on roles what Jung would call archetypes, one of which is the rescuer. Responders on call for local fires and national disasters, like the September 11th attack, also can embody the rescuer role.

In the case of September 11th, experts, it turns out, greatly overestimated the number of people in New York who would need rescuing from their emotional distress. Therapists by the dozens volunteered their services to New Yorkers after the towers fell, and, while some benefited, others were annoyed and one commentator referred the therapists' response as trauma tourism. It turns out people are far more resilient in disasters than experts thought. Granted, there had never been a 9-11 so there was no way to estimate the response other than comparing it with earthquakes and other trauma. A case study that surprised me found that first responders such as firefighters had post-traumatic stress disorder rates close to only ten percent. Also, the study couldn't really tell if people had been helped by the mental health providers, but the *providers felt great about it.* Helping can be healing. One of the best cures for depression is getting out and doing something for others. Hurricanes, floods, earthquakes and other disasters remind us that Mother Nature can be fickle. We are all dependent upon one another.

What does all of this have to do with the bunny nest I found in our backyard? Disaster responders, mental health ones in particular, may overdo it and rescue beyond what Mother Nature intended. I was guilty of over-rescuing, as you'll see, at my house.

I had just had a session with a new client who had some intense family issues; both parents had recently died and he was in a bitter, ugly, legal dispute with a family member. His story had an orphan quality and I was thinking about it while walking in our backyard shortly after his session when I nearly stepped on a fresh baby bunny hidden in the grass. Although its eyes were open I was at first not sure it was alive. I worried that it had lost its mother, would be eaten by a coyote, hit by the lawnmower. It was an orphaned bunny. Maybe it was just resting like a turtle does on its way out of the sea when it travels to lay its eggs. What was the message of this little bunny frozen in the grass? I have learned from watching the deer come and go from our property that they often have an affinity with certain clients, greeting them in a way at our driveway or standing guard outside my office as I work. It is almost as if some clients have a personal totem animal in the yard. Was this my client's totem animal? Was the bunny scared?

The day before I had read a piece in the paper that was a good reminder about how we often attempt to save animals from the wild when they don't need our help. The attempt does them more harm than good. Animals have instincts to find their own way. I would never pick up this bunny and put it in a shoe box like a doll and turn it into a pet project. It is the same with humans I often have to remember when they are in my consultation room. They have to find their own way. People often do not need to be rescued. If we over-rescue, they never find their own truth, their own power. We easily can end up being like a TV pyschologist, whose insistent telling others what to do could be robbing them of their own power. I went back later that day and the bunny was gone—eaten or alive I'll never know. Leave the rabbit in the wild. It will figure out what to do. The rabbit was only the beginning of life lessons on our land.

Another bunny encounter came in late July. For a week

we had been watching a rabbit hang out in the tall grasses of our fire pit circle—great place for hiding from predators we thought. Next, we found a burrowed hole beside a large stone in the fire pit, the grass loosely piled on top. Nearly stepping on it, we pulled the grass up to see little creatures huddled together in the dark barrow. *Mice* I thought. *Great, just what we need near the house.* Without my asking my husband to do something this time, but knowing I was distraught over rodent issues, he attempted to drown them in the hole. Luckily, they survived the flooding and within a few days the ears that I thought were mice suddenly started to look like bunny ears. Whew! Maybe they're only rabbits. I can live with that. The mother would occasionally pretend to be nonchalant and come by and sit on top of the hole to feed them and keep them warm. But she never stayed long. When a deer came close, she stood guard waiting to see what would happen.

We made the mistake of pulling up the grass cover one day to find a startled bunny jumping out. I became frantic that he would be eaten by crows and predators because he was out of the nest too soon. Awhile later the grass cover was mysteriously back on top. The next day the rabbits were all gone, no signs of disruption. I prayed of course that they made it out alive and into the forest like the young birds had from our deck. The rabbits were young, innocent and vulnerable in the big forest.

My next lesson in the cycle of life came from observing a bird's nest. We had a fuchsia plant hanging outside the back door of our house. It had become a nest for some baby birds and it was fascinating to watch the parents fly in and out warming and feeding the birds. I remarked at how busy that momma bird is feeding those babies. My husband had to point out early on that there wasn't just one bird flying in and out, but two! The father is involved and helping as well, he said! Turns out the male bird is a Mr. Mom. A sign of changing times, or has it always been this way in Mother Nature?

About a week into watching the birds dig up worms
and feed the little beaks popping out from the nest, I was
horrified to come out one day and see a struggling, under-
developed baby bird flailing on the deck not far from the
plant nest. I immediately cried out to my husband who
came running. I was distraught; I have always had a hard
time feeling the pain of animals and sometimes humans
around me. My husband scooped the bird up in a cloth at
my insistence to do something. It was a classic scene of the
woman, me, asking the guy to do something, anything,
so that she wouldn't have to be in discomfort. My husband quickly put the bird back in the nest and immediately regretted it, remembering something from his youth
about how birds would throw out the weak or deformed
from the nest. The deformed bird was now on top of the
other birds and was suffocating them. It was survival of
the fittest and a natural part of the animal world cycle. We
had disrupted it.

My husband went back in, tipped the plant, and took
the dying bird out to our ancestor stone in our garden, a
little shrine where we light a candle now and then for those
who have passed over. Would human scent be detected in
the nest by the parent birds? Would the parents abandon
the nest? Those were now our fears. It was a tense ten minutes, but the parents did return and feed their baby birds
again and again though now one of the birds was on the
edge of the plant nest. How would it stay warm? Was the
plan to push this one off the nest, as well? We don't know
the ways of nature. I believe it really isn't our business to
know it all, either. A week later, we watched three healthy
little birds follow a parent hopping from the nest by the
door to the edge of the forest. They had not flown but
hopped down from the nest.

In early spring, the frogs reappeared. The pond in our
backyard is soothing but I have come to dread attempting to fall asleep to the sound of lone frogs singing in

the middle of the night to attract a mate. Why not just sleep with the noise? With an open window I hear crickets and the sounds of my youth. Frogs are pretty loud and I would love to find a peaceful way to coexist with them. My husband has become quite the expert at catching frogs at night with a flashlight. He scores oh so many points by catching frogs to assure a quiet night's sleep. We bring them to the wetlands in front of the house where they can sing to their heart's content.

One night my husband went out to catch the loner frog croaking, but, instead, found a bullfrog. Our neighbors once had a huge one in their pond. Freddy is what they called him. Freddy had eaten all the beautiful koi fish in their pond so he was not their friend. They did not allow Freddy to live, which disturbed me. But Freddy's brother had now settled in our pond. What a great catch! Freddy's brother was immediately taken to the front of the wetlands. Only later did we realize that maybe Freddy had been eating all the little frogs! That was why it had been so quiet in recent weeks and my husband had not had to be up frog catching! Too late we realized we might have once again messed unwisely with nature. Freddy's sibling had showed up to help us out. I had been silently visualizing the frogs going to the front of our property and had hoped for relief from the incessant noise of croaking! And the help had come in the form of a Freddy, but we had him removed! Snakes like to eat frogs. Maybe that could be a solution.

I'm not afraid of snakes. I have not encountered a rattlesnake yet so I may be speaking prematurely. So when I saw the snakes hanging out around our fountain I was fascinated. I saw a kaleidoscope of colorful snakes in our backyard one sunny afternoon by the pond. I spotted a green garden snake's tail and then saw a flash of yellow. Upon closer look, I found two snakes entangled. Soon another yellow one appeared and joined the mix, twisting and turning around and around each other. They moved so fast, I wasn't sure if now there were three snakes twisting amongst the rocks and pond. Had I just witnessed a snake birth? I wasn't sure. I know they shed their skins, which I have seen before, but this was a whole different dance. The symbol of the snake eating its tail came to mind—symbol of the unity of all things and linked to the philosopher's stone, truly a symbol of rebirth if there ever was one.

Years ago we found a cat in our backyard meowing in pain. Her hind legs were broken, having been attacked, we believe, by a coyote. Brewster barked at the cat. That's why it hid in the crawl space under the deck of our home. Later, we found her again. She had moved herself on her front legs to a sunny spot in the woodshed. We put her in a box and took her to the local vet. We wanted to put the cat out of its misery. Sometimes rescuing is done with pure heart and good intentions. I am always struck by animals when they are dying or decide it is time to die. They do it all on their own. They just crawl into the wood, no tubes, respiratory support or hospice. Would that cat have preferred to die in pain under the deck or in the open air and sunshine? Maybe. It might have been all about my inability to witness her suffering.

I hate to watch anything suffer, but nature will take care of its own if we just stay out of the way. Nature is wise beyond our knowing. All we have to do is just stand back and let the cycles of birth and death continue without our interference. As a therapist I have to remember the lessons of nature and keep my over-rescuer in check. If a client comes in, ambivalent and on the fence about a relationship, for instance, I will most likely play the witness to their story. I don't believe in giving advice but in guiding others to find their own answers. As a facilitator, I am there to ask questions, explore and examine feelings and thoughts. To discover with them what the soul needs. I am not in the business of affirming or making decisions for them and nature is a good reminder of that.

There is a Nordic rune that says, "Focus on what is coming to be and what is passing away." I like that philosophy. My learnings about life, death and rebirth have extended beyond pets to my own backyard. The cycles of life seen in the bunnies, bees, frogs and snakes on our three acres remind me that there is so much we can learn through the simple observation of animals.

Whether my husband and I are encountering bunnies, birds, frogs or snakes around our house, we always feel fortunate that we get to observe the cycles of life, death and rebirth through their coming and going. We hear often the howling of coyotes and the calling of owls at midnight. Lingering deer seem to find safety in the shadow of our house. Too bad we don't have enough time for ants, bees, butterflies and dragonflies. Our backyard is teeming with life—and death. We had to learn, though, to leave well enough alone in nature and not to rescue. Observing what is dying and being reborn right around our house keeps the messages from nature close to home. Spring is the season of birth and renewal, in summer life is at its peak, in the fall it is time for harvest, and during the dark winter months the natural cycle of death prepares for rebirth. There is just no way to avoid death. It is the same for us, in our lifecycle, and for our pets in their shorter lifespan. The animals in our backyard have made me reflect about the never-ending cycle of life and have fostered in me a deep love for Mother Nature.

So how do we face mortality and death, especially of those we love? Dogs are part of the animal kingdom, close to nature, and they help us transition in life from child to adult and from birth to death. They show us the way to die with courage and dignity. They don't want to stick around too long in pain. Brewster seemed to have lost control of his bladder near the end. But on the morning the vet came to put him to sleep, we saw him stand in between our two backyards and clearly pee in front of us all. He looked straight at us as if to say, "See, I have control of my bladder. I just wanted you to know it was my time. I want to go home."

Have you ever seen an injured animal in nature prepare to die? It curls up into a ball and wants to be left alone. No fuss, no protesting. It accepts death as just another part of having been alive.

Second Mitzie Dream

The second dream I had about Mitzie I have titled *"Burying Her Brush"* and it was probably the most vivid one I had of her. While cleaning out my parents' attic, I came across an old brown Eagles branded grocery bag. I was in such a nonstop whirlwind of sorting, purging, and throwing boxes down the attic stairs, I hardly paused until I came across this bag. I didn't know what was inside, but the moment I unfolded the creases and even before I had peered into the dark interior, I knew what lay inside: Mitzie's belongings. The scent of her lingered in the air and I felt tears run down my cheeks. Her yellow bowl, newspaper toy, brown leash, and brown brush lay inside. Later, her orange plastic bed tub came down from the attic, too. My mother had saved nearly everything we didn't sell at our one and only garage sale. This was one bag I was so glad she kept all those years. Fast forward many years—and I still had Mitzie's vintage brown, wooden-handled bristle brush with me. Mitzie's brown brush that was used on her brindle coat sparked a dream and a synchronistic healing, bringing in other members of the animal kingdom.

I thought about the brush one day when I talked with a woman in a store who told me a story about her dog passing over. She was having a hard time letting go of her dog. A friend said she needed to grieve and that her holding on was keeping her dog from moving on in heaven. Her story about her deceased beloved dog stayed with me and I had a second dream about Mitzie days later.

Dreams of our beloved pets can come out of the blue and bring comfort, as mine did many years after Mitzie's death. Mitzie had a sunbathing spot at the southwest corner of our family house. She loved it there. Mom tried to plant flowers, but Mitzie dug them up and reclaimed her spot every time.

I'm in the backyard of our childhood home and Mitzie is sunbathing. It's like I am still a kid and small enough to crouch down into the basement eave directly behind her sunbathing spot and see through the half windows into our basement. I don't think it's safe for her because a deer is nosing around, so I lead her to the other, northeast side of the house. But the house is now the one I currently live in as an adult in Washington. The spot I've led her to is just outside my window in the bedroom where I'm dreaming. Mitzie curls up; peaceful above ground in the northeast spot, but the deer finds her and stands above her just before Mitzie is to be lowered into the ground. I want her to stay hovered like a cloud at ground level, not below. I try to move the deer's leg, but the deer is stubborn and will not move. Somewhere inside, I know it's for our own good that it won't move, because Mitzie needs to go into the ground. Mitzie is being buried, I thought, and the deer is guiding the way.

In part, because of this dream, I decided to dig out Mitzie's things, now stored in my garage. The smell was still fresh as I took out Mitzie's brown-handled brush, once again bringing tears to my eyes. *I should bury this in the woods*, I thought, as a symbolic dog memorial of some sort.

Mitzie in the garden

The brush would symbolize releasing Mitzie and letting go of any subconscious part of her I may have been holding onto. I knew the special spot I would place it and one day took my part-time neighbor's dog Brewster along with me to do it.

We walked out to the woods, Brewster, as always, happy to be going on an adventure with me. As I knelt and dug a hole, Brewster watched quietly. When I placed the brush in the ground, he stood with all four legs over the hole as I put the dirt back in.

I was shocked. Brewster was acting just the way the deer did in my dream. Neither would move or budge. Brewster stood guard over the whole process of my burying Mitzie's brush, just as the deer presided over Mitzie being lowered into the ground. I got a sense he thought this was his duty somehow. Even as we turned to go, he stood a moment longer and then followed me out. I found it interesting that Brewster in my backyard ritual had taken the place of the deer in my dream in guarding Mitzie's spirit.

The dream shows how my nostalgic clinging to the past around Mitzie is keeping both of us from moving on. Mitzie needs to go on to the next dimension and I have to let her go emotionally and allow her to be buried.

Deer in our backyard

Later that day, deer showed up in our backyard for twenty minutes and circled the entire house, eating, walking, and lying for hours. They stayed longer that day than any other time I had witnessed in our many years at the house. They were there to help me process my dream about deer and dog. I went back a few days later and the dirt was as I had left it, not unturned as I had feared, that an animal would smell the brush's scent.

I found my dream about Mitzie's brush and the deer to be reassuring. It showed me that I would move through my grief if I could let go and "bury" her, so to speak. It's clear that the brush and deer were symbolic messages around letting go of Mitzie. In my life's book, the deer is an archetypal symbol of the wounded feminine and appears at synchronistic moments in my life. Obviously an important message was struggling to release itself from my unconscious. It was the same message the woman in the store shared: bury, grieve and let go of your pets so they can move on, too.

Burying Mitzie's brush was a profound experience. Next time I'll imagine doing a ritual for my old stuffed animal Spot that has gotten many extra spots over the years symbolizing even more of my past.

Brewster's Graduation

The night after Brewster's passing, another healing dream came to me. As I just told you, Brewster played the role of a protective guardian angel helping me bury Mitzie's brush in the forest. In this dream Brewster moves on to help others with his protective presence and play an even bigger role in heaven.

I first met a beagle from the Himalayans who was to be my dream guide in the animal kingdom. I feel that I was, in a way, privileged to witness Brewster's life review as a dog. I saw two streams of pure, bright, white lights, the most beautiful I had ever seen, running in parallel semicircles to each other. It was like a Pisces sign without the horizontal mark but longer. The lights had a brilliance that was not of this world. It is hard to find words to describe this dream as it felt as if everything in the animal kingdom was telepathic and any message or knowing was transmitting immediately within. There was no hell, as in the Christian Bible, or bardo, as in the Tibetan Book of the Dead.

The two bright streams of light glimmered and seemed to be telling me that Brewster (Big B) would move on in its the next level. B was thrilled, honored, and humbled to be given an overseer-like role for a small part of the animal kingdom. He would be "doing rounds from above," similar to when he did protective rounds of both our yards to make sure all was well.

He always was a great Shepherd. Now he got a new flock to supervise. Other animals were so happy about Brewster's new place. They felt taken care of with B in this position. It felt as if he was playing some kind of a good shepherd role in the animal kingdom. B had graduated to the next level.

Also, Brewster, without words, told me in the dream how we not only received gifts from him, but gave him something that helped him grow, too. He had grown from hanging out with my husband and me around our kind of mysticism. It was like a telepathic exchange, so words can't even describe what I was feeling and sensing in the dream. It was helping him grow and move to the next level. There was a feeling of mutual gratitude passing instantaneously that needed no verbal expression. I silently expressed my gratitude to him for all he has done to heal my heart.

Brewster got his loving temperament, sense of unconditional love, discipline and hard work from his owners. They created a base from which he could serve and share his love with others. He was always ready to "work" with our neighbor who instilled in him his loyalty and dedication. It was a privilege for me to be able to see how Brewster was doing and how life transitions and ends in the animal kingdom. In the dream, I was like a witness to his review because we were close. So it felt as if I was given this gift of seeing his light shining so brightly and beautifully. In the animal kingdom, everything is so simple, direct, and focused. There is no waste of mental words or complicated life reviews. Brewster was happy, thrilled, at peace and in the right place. I felt nothing but pure joy and celebration for him. How could I grieve my missing him when he was in such a beautiful place, serving above? Brewster had taught me about giving and receiving.

Upon awakening I felt my gratitude for all that he had done for me the past years. He really helped me heal in many matters of the heart, particularly my inner child, with all the times he had intuited that I needed some company, and the times I spent walking with him. I cherished those times.

The dream surprisingly left me in somewhat of a celebratory mood. I felt happy and thrilled for him. I felt peace in my heart. I basked in the light's beauty and the privilege of witnessing how it works in a kingdom other than my own. The brightness and brilliance stayed with me all through the next day. It was closest thing I've ever experienced to visiting the other side and I was feeling its lasting effects.

Later in the week, while meditating outside about B's passing, I gazed upon a star and thought of my dream. I couldn't hear the jingle of his collar but felt he could still be around somehow, and that I could remember him by looking up at the stars. Since stars twinkle in the heavens, the star symbolized Brewster being upstairs in heaven shining down on us here on earth. It's been five years since Brewster died and I still miss him. Once in a while when I go to get the morning paper I think of him. As I write this around Christmas, I look out of my window and see the three large stars that light up high in the top of three trees in our backyard. They shine for our ancestors and for the guardians of our land. Brewster has among them a place of honor.

Pet Visitations

Where do dogs go when they die? Most of us who have had a pet that died will have wondered if pets go to heaven. I don't want to go into doctrines of religion. While writing this chapter it seemed the present Pope had made remarks while comforting a boy whose dog had died, indicating, "One day, we will see our animals again in eternity with Christ. Paradise is open to all of God's creatures." Later this remark was denied by the Vatican, but maybe the Pope, whose name is Francis, could consult his namesake of Assisi who is the patron saint of animals. No doubt, the Saint could tell what he sees around him.

Anyway I have my own experience and sometimes clients have shared their stories about what happens to their pets when they die. I can't imagine a heaven without Mitzie. Is it possible there would be a heaven with majestic trees and the lion lying with the lamb without dogs in the background? Hardly possible as I believe animals have souls.

I believe they go to a heavenly place and are there on the other side waiting for us when we make our way to our final resting place. I've decided that dogs live in a holographic memory state. The dog images and symbols reside in our collective unconscious: an archaic vacuum common to us all that holds the memories of everything that ever happened. All our loved ones, including our pets, are there to tap into at any time the spirit moves us.

Loss is something we can't avoid in life. I like to think our pets may come back to visit us after they die to help us cope with losses in life. One of my clients, Rose, when she was a kid had a dog named Alvin. "The other dogs in the neighborhood didn't like him, but I thought he was great," Rose said. "He used to sleep with me every night and cuddle up next to my left hip. He died when I was eight and I missed him terribly."

When Rose's cat, Tabitha, became ill, memories flooded back of losing Alvin. The vet told her Tabitha would be gone by afternoon, but the cat held on and so Rose's family decided to let her sleep that last night at home.

That night, Rose had the most vivid dream that Alvin was with her in bed. She woke up her husband. "Alvin is here," she told him, knowing in her heart Alvin had come to take Tabitha home. That next morning, her cat died and they took her to be cremated, glad they had kept her with them overnight.

She had heard that when a loved one passes on, an ancestor from the other side comes to take the deceased back home. Similarly, our former pets that have passed on seem to come back to take our dying pets home to the light. Rose shared, "My grandpa saw his favorite dog, Scruffy, come for him. Grandmother said she saw a dog's shadow come through the hallway the night he died." Pet visitations gave Rose a great source of comfort during the loss of not only Tabitha, but her grandfather, too.

Another client, Connie, was struggling with the topic of death and what happens when we die. Natural disasters in the news had left her with unexplained, intrusive, worrisome thoughts about losing her loved ones. Under hypnosis, Connie went back to her first experience with death at the tender age of six. In a hushed whisper, she shared, "I'm barefoot and playing with my friend in our backyard. My parents' mean tenant, who lives behind our house, is yelling at us as we run around in circles. She has two scary Doberman dogs."

Connie recalled how the following scene unfolded. She remembered seeing her mother at the back door holding her little brother who had slipped and fallen, leaving the door ajar. Her mother wasn't able to hold both her brother and their dog, a little Yorkie named Heathcliff. The dog ran out into the yard before her mother could stop him. Connie watched in horror as the Dobermans attacked little Heathcliff, killing him before her eyes. She remembered hearing her little brother cry as she felt tears rolling down her face.

The next scene she recalled was standing in the yard with her family. Everyone was crying, even her father. She had never seen her dad cry before. Afterward, she realized this was her first experience with death and a traumatic one at that. No wonder she had a fear of death suddenly ripping her away from loved ones. "Our pets never really leave us," I suggested. "Their essence lives on." The next week she brought in a picture of her Heathcliff. It was December, so together with her children, she honored Heathcliff's memory by putting his name on a stocking and hanging it on her fireplace mantle.

Ashes to Ashes

We will all become forefathers and mothers by and by. I recently read a book on sacred dying and it made me realize that one of the benefits of having dogs is that they taught me not just the sacredness of life, but how to die with dignity as well. Because they have a shorter life span, it's reasonable to think that they will pass over before we do. I know that will be a comfort someday if I'm lying on my deathbed and feeling scared about dying. I know they will be waiting for me on the other side. They will be there to greet me just like they always did in life. Their eyes will be smiling, their tails wagging, and their hearts open, welcoming me in abundant joy. They can't wait to see me. Sometimes it seems that I feel closer to Mitzie since she died. She is in me and will always be a part of me; a part of that greater collective unconscious.

I will finally get to smell Mitzie for real again, pet her short little brown hairs, and walk around the block with her as many times as I want. All the other part-time pets and rent-a-dogs will be there. Oscar will fly over and sit on my head, helping me with the transition in a way only a special parakeet like Oscar can. I won't be alone. The pets will be with me every step of the way. Even though they are crossing over from another kingdom, they will be there when I drift and float out of the tunnel that connects me from this earthly life to the other. My client Rose's pet visitation dream and her father seeing Scruffy, has convinced me of that. Our beloved pets will be part of the welcome-home committee. Instead of a neighborhood welcome wagon committee, it's more like a welcome pet community.

There are many ways we can die. We never know. I could fall flat from a heart attack tomorrow. A loved one could be hooked up to life support which makes for a totally different kind of goodbye. But if one knows one is near the end—perhaps one has only a few hours, days or weeks, maybe even months—what would make the experience a sacred one?

Bringing in someone's pillow and bedding to a hospital room can make a dying person feel more at ease. Making the bed and room as personal and cozy as possible is key. Let's not forget pain management as part of the equation to make one as comfortable as can be expected. Some like last rites, or having family and friends around. Others want a favorite food to eat or a passage read to them.

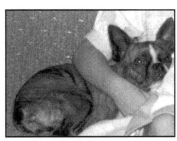

Mitzie snuggle

What would I want around me if I were dying? I guess I have never thought about what I would like or need in my final hours before dying. A pet could help. My loved ones would be a part of that picture, of course, in the last moments, forming a circle around me. I imagine I would want music, candles, mementos, and framed pictures. One of Mitzie would be a comfort. My ancestors could be on the other side as part of the welcoming committee. Pictures of them also may be of comfort. In addition, I'd want a room with lots of windows to look out into the world. For myself, I would like to recreate a little room in the lake house I always loved: the orange bedspread, night table, the sounds of crickets through an open window and the sounds of the lake water lapping up against the shore. Pomegranate juice, crackers and a journal would be nice, provided I can still drink, eat, write or talk. Talking is comforting, and if I had a pet, I would want it there curled up next to me, too.

If I were in the hospital, I would ask someone to smuggle in a dog if I had one and if it was small enough. Some say the love and support a pet can provide when someone is dying is exceptional. A pet could help ease the way to death, though it would be harder, perhaps, for the animal once you're gone. Animals don't hold back on grieving from what I see, and that would be comforting.

But life is fleeting and why concern myself with a picture that takes me out of the present? Who knows what the circumstances of our deaths will be? It's a heavy thought for sure, one I don't want to dwell on too long, just as I don't believe in dwelling on past lives for too long. I don't see how it is a good idea; it only takes me out of the present life. I believe those greater unknown mysteries for a reason. I try to live life on a need to know basis.

Why insult the divine by trying to control what will be the ultimate letting go of control? But this book and writing about death and pets as master therapists has made me ponder not only what I would want, but what my loved ones may want, how I can create a sacred space for them in their final hours or days.

Memorabilia

Mitzie look-alike

Our living room was a kind of shrine to Boston Terriers. My mother had a collection of Boston Terrier curios that we had given her over the years starting when Mitzie was still alive. We have the life-size porcelain Boston Terrier that was the *creme de la creme* of the collection. She stood next to the fake palm tree in the corner. I thought it was too funny to have our dog pose next to the porcelain version as you can see the photo below. I remember Mitzie being so patient posing for me as I took that picture. She seems to be looking at me saying to herself, *"I'm doing this just to amuse you Karen, you know I love you unconditionally and would do just about anything for you....and a Wishbone dog treat."*

We have the Christmas ornament stash as well. I have Boston Terrier dog ornaments hanging on my Christmas tree every year in all manner and forms. Bostons are wrapped under the tree and in stockings and with wings and halos—little ones, big ones, flat ones, homemade ones (my favorite). Just about any kind of Boston ornament you can imagine has been on one of our family trees. Our dog was brindle, as I mentioned, and these imitations are black-and-white, so I have to use my imagination to see them as an embodiment of our dog. My mother has received any number of Boston Christmas gifts: a blanket, a door knocker, a coat hook, stickers, key chains, and T-shirts.

Other than ornaments, I have an antique, door-stopper Boston Terrier. I had it in storage for quite some time. I probably didn't want our rent-a-dogs to get confused by it, thinking it might be a real dog and that they weren't our number one favorite. Over the years, with eBay and the popularity of Bostons, the gift choices have improved. It has become a ritual of sorts to see who will find the best Boston Christmas gift for my parents. Whether this is healthy or not is the subject of another article. The best was the year my sister and I both gave my mother Boston Terrier purses. Neither of us knew what the other had gotten for mother, of course. The funny thing was, one was obviously more of an adult dog and the other more of a puppy. It was representative of our birth order who gave her which purse. My mother thought it was hilarious. I think we all got a few good laughs out of those gifts.

Over the years, my husband has gotten used to this family ritual. At first, it seemed bizarre to him and I don't think he quite understood what the whole fuss was about.

Now he joins in the mayhem, keeping an eye out for Boston paraphernalia.

Boston knick-knacks

Does anyone else do this? Is my family just crazy or trapped in the Boston past? Are we trying to bury unfinished grief in a pile of mementos? Will there be a time when we are just done with it all?

Or run out of fun Boston gifts? Who does this kind of knick-knacking celebratory ritual over a dog's memory? Is it healthy? Or is it just a sign that my family is dog-crazy and confirms what I've known all along?

You know something must be off in your inner world when you actually stockpile Boston gifts in your closet and find yourself in July perusing eBay for a Christmas gift, hoping to locate someone who has that just-right, antique Boston for sale after cleaning out the garage! There are so many memorabilia for sale. We can't be the only ones with this eccentric behavior!

Maybe we will tire of it and put it all up and sell it as one big lot on eBay. I have seen that kind of thing before. There does come a time when we are just done with a collection and clutter. I have read Peter Walsh's books on clutter and imagine he would tell me to stop, if I am done with collecting Bostons, to take a picture and sell them all—just like that. I know I'm not alone, thanks to eBay. I knew a woman who cleaned out her garage and couldn't give away hundreds of Beanie Babies. That could be me with Boston paraphernalia someday!

Maybe dogs aren't meant to be memorialized like humans. What are the stages of grief we go through when losing a pet as a kid? Are they the same as for an adult? Elizabeth Kubler Ross lists them as: denial, anger, bargaining, depression, and acceptance.[5]

I think I got stuck somewhere between denial and depression, with partial acceptance. The story goes that, as children, we had a pet turtle for a short time. It lived in a fish tank and we were fond of it. When it died, we buried it in our backyard. Mitzie went out there and dug it up. So much for pet memorials. We never had a funeral for our dog; hence, here I am writing this book.

In how many ways can you eulogize a dog?

Memorials

A family mourns its pet in this 19th-century photo from the White River Museum

How do we let go of beloved pets?

The White River Valley Museum in Auburn, Washington, had a museum exhibit called "Dead: Unearthing the Shift in Funerary Practices From Home to Mortuary." In the past, families prepared their loved one's body to display in the home for guests to visit and for burial. They were more used to being around the bodies of the deceased, since people often died at home. Crematoriums weren't big in those days, either. Death was more real.

Family members cared for their loved ones up until their final breath. Clocks were stopped, mirrors were turned, windows were covered during a memorial, and women wore black for a year. Undertakers were more like salesmen and had lots of extras, in addition to coffins, to offer. And therefore, with their pets, it wasn't unusual to have a memorial photograph taken of a beloved pet surrounded by mourners. It is fascinating to see how families mourned pets in the nineteenth century. They didn't have grief counselors in those days. Hospices and mortuaries weren't prevalent then. It may sound a bit morbid from our modern-day perspective to have a picture taken with your dead pet before it is put in the ground.

Dog Casket, 2300 BC Turkey

Nowadays, we don't think of putting our pets in coffins. It sounded downright strange, but maybe it wasn't such a bad idea, because people were sure to acknowledge the loss and mourn together. In ancient times, pet memorials were approached differently. This is a photo of a dog casket from a royal family in ancient Turkey dated 2300 BC. Pets were obviously part of the family and memorized even back then judging by the elaborate engraved pet casket.

Angel Wings

One of my goals for writing this book (other than convincing my husband that we need to get a dog) is that Mitzie will get her angel wings and her soul will be free from any earthly attachments that might have been holding her down here. Working with her memory has been like peeling an onion. There is layer upon layer. Mitzie represents some layers deep down in my unconscious: the fear of abandonment, the transference in relationships, and the willingness to let go of the ghosts of the past. I think she already has her angel wings; at least I see them on her when I look at the ornament on my Christmas tree of the Boston with wings. The thought makes me smile.

As I've mentioned, I think dogs live in this holographic kind of vacuum we can tap into at any time. It holds a memory of our pets and loved ones who have passed over. I can tap into that memory state just by smelling Mitzie's old leash, feeling the wool on the green winter vest my mother sewed for her, which I also have, or remembering her now-buried brush.

Mitzie has passed over and moved farther on since I buried her brush and the deer stood over it in my dream. Grief has been replaced by vivid, fond memories that bring a smile to my face. I can imagine her looking back at me and smiling with her ears down, little tail wagging. We can't hold on too tightly to our pets or rent-a-pets that have passed over. I learned through my dreams of Mitzie and Brewster that they had work to do on the other side, and letting go of their memories helped not only me, but them, to move on.

Mitzie, as well as all my part-time and rent-a-dogs and bird, have taught me to stay connected to heaven as well as earth. They also have encouraged me to stay in the present moment like dogs so easily do. They jump for toys, stare off into space, roll in the grass, and really feel each moment. I wanted to circle the rug like Mitzie did and curl up next to a heater, too! Dogs give you a steady, unconditional, constant presence you can't find anywhere else—that is, unless you have a "dog with tears" like my husband at home!

This year I have ordered something different for my family for Christmas. I have the usual Boston fun gift for my mother: a linseed-filled Boston Terrier door stopper. I even found matching Boston Terrier sweaters at Kohl's, went all out, and got one for each of the women in the family.

Next year, I think it's time to put Mitzie to rest properly, something we should have done years ago. That means having a proper funeral for her. I was inspired by hearing my sister order a plaque for their beloved Dash for their backyard. "I got one for Oreo and, by gosh, told my family we were going to the backyard to honor Oreo's memory with the plaque even though we've been putting it off." She said it wasn't going to be like Mitzie, where we never had closure. "We have Dash's ashes and will do the same for him."

Way to go! I was impressed she was changing history by creating a memorial for her two precious Havanese dogs that had crossed over. It's understandable that circumstances differ from how it was with Mitzie. Back then, people just buried their pets in their backyard or brought it to the vet. Nobody in our neighborhood had pet urns or got the ashes from the veterinarian's office. Nor was it like the Victorian age where dogs were memorialized in the home with photographs. Times have changed and dogs that have always been like family are honored the way we honor loved ones who have died today. My neighbors closed off Brewster's doggie door in their garage and added a small shelf inside where they placed Brewster's urn. It reminded me of an altar shrine I might see in a church, except it wasn't a church but Brewster's old home in their garage. Dogs are our teachers and masters at therapy. As we grow and evolve, how we see our pets grows and evolve as well.

Oreo's farewell

Why not create the same closure for Mitzie, I thought? I'll fire up a clay memorial plaque and we can all go outside into my mother's garden and give Mitzie a proper funeral and find some closure. Maybe we can join hands and sing "Kumbaya," especially the lyrics about crying, and laugh about how we have remembered her since her passing. Maybe I'll even bury a copy of this book in Mitzie's spot along with her brown jingly collar, yellow bowl, bones, a coat, and toy we saved all these years. I'll keep her brown leather leash, as I have used it over the years to walk my part-time and rent-a-dogs. It's a better way to keep her memory alive down through pet generations than trapped in the basement of my subconscious mind where it longs for release.

What I wish for you is that you find ways to honor your pet's passing. If an anniversary of your pet is approaching, take a moment to remember what a blessing your pet was in your life, your family's life, and the lives of all those it touched. Fill in some of the questions provided in the final section and create a crying container if you need to. Over time, learn to find ways to let go and move on. Don't make the mistake my family made the first time around and not create closure through a dog memorial.

A Letter of Apology to Mitzie

Memorializing a pet is a personal matter. In trying to make peace with my past, I wrote a letter of apology to Mitzie. It just seemed fitting.

I'm sorry, Mitzie, for dressing you up like a bride and making you marry Buffy, the neighbor dog. You two weren't really even friends and yet you lived kitty-corner from each other. Buffy was a big, fluffy dog who spent most of his time in a fenced-in patio in the neighbor's backyard. Just because you were a girl and he was a boy, you were suddenly stuck with each other on a sunny afternoon, surrounded by kids in a make-believe church made out of lawn chairs put on their sides sufficing for a wall, a sheet serving as a rooftop. You had to walk down the aisle we created for you. Luckily, they didn't sell all those wild dog outfits when I was a child or we would have had you in a white one!

We made a garland out of white lawn flowers for you. You were a stubborn dog, a Taurus through and through. And I know you didn't want to wear the flower wreath we tried to put on your head. Sorry about that. We had a fresh-

ly picked bouquet of yellow daisies, too, but you had no hands to hold them with, only paws. Thanks for putting up with us.

Sorry for pulling your little tail and tormenting you to the point you nipped at me. I deserved that one. I'm sorry my parents had to talk about the possibility doing something about you because of MY allergies. Sorry you couldn't come into our bedrooms and sleep at the bottom of our beds in your later years. We loved you, it was the only way to keep you and not have to give you away.

Sorry we put you into the crazy dog swing we made for you on our swing set. You were so patient with us, which is a Taurus virtue you brilliantly displayed that sunny June afternoon. It was hot and you're a dog, but we had you wrapped up in all these blankets around a swing like there was no tomorrow. I thought you hated it, but come to find out after sharing memories with my sister that she thought you loved it. Your head would bob back and forth with the swing, lulling you into a hypnotic state. I look at the pictures and think how thoroughly bored with it all you were. But there you sit, patiently waiting—or maybe it was just too far for you to jump out without breaking your neck. We will never know.

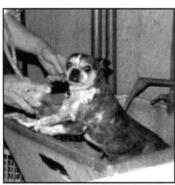
Mitzie's spa time

How about bath time? Did you always love it? If we said the words, "Mitzie take a bath," you would go stand at the top of the stairs ready to go downstairs to the sink for your spa time. Do all dogs love baths, perhaps? You probably weren't typical in that it was really a favorite pastime. I can see the pink hose and your cute little paws up on the edge of the gray sink, shivering at first until the water warmed up, your big *grey eyes looking at us like, "Ahhh, spa time." You would come out of a fresh bath ready to be cuddled up in a towel.*

On the other hand, if we were getting ready to go on a trip and got out the suitcases you were out there in the car making sure you would not be left behind and sometimes you would start to shake if you thought we might come to take you out of the backseat. You never really took off hiding or ran away from home. You loved car rides and racing in circles around the yard when our neighbor Mr. Heilman was out. You also loved Grandma's farm, playing tug of war when we came home, your corner, Milk Bone Dog Biscuits, the heater vent in the kitchen, pulling up the kitchen rug into a ball to sleep on, naps, Christmas stocking goodies, walks, and bike rides in your basket.

Writing my letter of apology began as a way to process my years with Mitzie and put to rest any guilty feelings I might have been harboring. It became a healing trip down memory lane reviewing favorite times with her.

Third Mitzie Dream

This was probably my most vibrant dream and is titled as *"Just One More Walk around the Block."*

In the dream, I'm taking Mitzie for one last walk around my childhood neighborhood block. She is beaming and so happy and so am I. It's so vivid; it's like she's alive again. This is a lucid dream because it feels so real; it's not an ordinary dream. Mitzie's on her brown leather leash. It's warm out, so she doesn't need her woolen jacket. We savor our walk all the way around the block; we don't take the short cut through the neighbor's yard but complete our circle. As we come around the bend and I see my childhood home in front of my eyes, I know I'm done and so is she. I can release her now.

I awake crying with joy, having gotten one final walk with Mitzie. Was that experience real? How do we know when an experience is real?

According to psychologist Carl C. G. Jung, "There are, and always have been, those who cannot help but see that the world and its experiences are in the nature of a symbol, and that it really reflects something that lies hidden in the subject himself, in his own trans-subjective reality."[6]

What this means to me is that the dog in this story is an old symbol reflecting what has been going on in my inner world. It is part, not only of my waking life, but, of my dream life as well and reflects the three stages—life, death, and rebirth—that we all experience. What I wish for you if you're reading this book and you currently have a pet, is that you can celebrate your pet's life each and every day. Take lots of pictures and make lasting memories with your pet. And if you dream about your pet, write your pet dreams down in a journal.

Rest in Peace

Pets help us come to terms with our own death, whether that is tomorrow or twenty or more years in the future. Their early death is often our first experience with death and initiates us into letting go of this earthly life. After writing this part of my book, I know what song I want played at my funeral. I can actually say I'm less fearful, or that there are fewer unknowns now when I die. I'm more comfortable with death and dying. I don't believe I have ever been really afraid of dying or the afterlife. I think I dread more the idea of being in pain, suffering or discomfort while dying. But that is why we have hospices and morphine.

There are fewer unknowns now when I die because I'm reassured that there will be a homecoming of some sort on the other side when I die. I will finally get to see Mitzie. One of the first things I want to do when I cross those pearly gates is take Mitzie for a walk around the block. I want to see Brewster and Oreo. But, mostly I want to see the family and friends who have passed over already. Also, I will get to see my ancestors. I'm especially curious to meet those I never met. My grandfathers I never got to meet. I will get to see them. So in a weird way there is something to look forward to around death.

Because I've had a pet and have processed its death in this book, I am more at peace around death and dying. Not just the death of beloved pets, but the death of my loved ones and my own inevitable death that I'll have to deal with someday myself. In the end that is one dance I'll ultimately do alone. When that is, I have no idea and I don't want to dwell on it, but I do know that pets have helped me move forward and have more peace and understanding. And it feels like I'm putting Mitzie to rest with every draft. And with every edit there is more and more peace between Mitzie and I.

Over the years, Mitzie has somehow become this holographic crystallized memory I lovingly put on our Christmas tree yearly—this spark of innocence and nostalgic memory of days long gone. In my dreams, Mitzie's image continued to stay alive and guide me in my unfinished mourning. So many people can relate to losing a pet. Pets live on in so many ways even long after they are gone. Maybe it's a reminder of a love that never dies. Even though I've missed Mitzie, we are still connected spiritually, as I see her in my dreams. It was as if I could feel, see, hear, and smell her essence in those dreams. She has become a kind of totem animal that is still friends with me. Mitzie modeled unconditional positive regard. She paved the way for my work as a therapist.

The director of many PBS documentaries, Ken Burns, said in the TV program *Finding Your Roots* that his mother's death paved the way for his career. From when he was the age of three his mother was stricken with breast cancer and he lived every day knowing she could be gone in an instant. She died when he was eleven. He credits his father-in-law, a psychologist, with an insight that reveals how his past paved the way for his present career. "He told me that my whole work was an attempt to make people, long gone, come back alive."[7] Perhaps that is what I have attempted to do with Mitzie. I've been unconsciously trying to bring her back to life through the pictures, Christmas ornaments and stories of my youth. She will always be, in my eyes, a master therapist. Maybe I could have saved years of therapy just by having another Boston Terrier. But I know it doesn't work that way. Pet transference could be a bit of a mess with another Boston Terrier on the scene and dogs can't talk to you about how the past has become the present. A therapist is helpful for that.

However, there are different styles of therapy for people just as there are different approaches within dog therapy. The pet-centered approach that Mitzie embodied taught me about staying grounded, listening to my intuition, being present, having empathy, being authentic and genuine, and, most important of all, about unconditional positive regard, better known as unconditional love. I like to think that Carl Rogers would be proud of Mitzie and all the permanent and part-time dogs I've had the pleasure of knowing. Maybe he is upstairs right now playing fetch and comparing notes with them.

Mitzie was consistent in all of Roger's person-centered psychology principles. She never went to graduate school or watched any of his training videos. Yet, she was a great master therapist in her own right. And it came from her own heart and inner knowing. I had no idea that dogs would end up being masters at teaching therapy or have their own pet-centered psychology. Day by day, year by year, I have come to understand that we can learn so much from the animal kingdom. Yes, Carl just might be proud of all the permanent and part-time dogs.

As I've said, I would like to have a permanent dog.

Funny thing is in Buddhist philosophy, permanence is something of a joke. Life is impermanent, and since dogs have considerably shorter lifespans than humans, we are reminded of our mortality whenever we have to say goodbye to a beloved pet. Perhaps, this makes us mindful to pay attention and appreciate the wonder, connections, and joy of every day.

I don't know if Buddha had any pets. I doubt it. But he did say something about life having three basic facts of existence: impermanence, suffering and non-self. I get that there is suffering in life and I'm still working on that non-self concept and will have to get back to you on that one. However, I've learned that this fact of impermanence is a helpful principle to keep in mind about having pets. All the time I've been wishing for my own dog, I also know that life is fleeting. Death can be beckoning behind any unknown door, so my time will be precious until it's time to say goodbye. In a strange way, I will always hold that role as a part-time caretaker and guardian pet owner lightly. The animals in my life are precious because they were never really mine in the first place. They were on loan to have and hold until death. I learned through the dream about Brewster how the animal kingdom quite possibly has its own guidelines, levels of hierarchy, and knowing that are different from the human kingdom.

I trust Mitzie is at peace upstairs, running free and happy as ever. As soon as I'm done down here in earth school and make my transition, I will be joining her for another walk around the block. In the meantime, I know that she is in the little haloed Boston Terrier angel Christmas ornament hanging in my tree. Our loved ones are as alive as we are, whether it is in our dreams or in the ornaments we hang in our Christmas trees. Mitzie is just around the next bend, ready to greet me with a wag of her tail and love in her eyes.

Part III

DOG

The Next Dog or Not?

One or Two?

"When a man's best friend is his dog, that dog has a problem."

—Edward Abbey

"No matter how little money and how few possessions you own, having a dog makes you rich."

—Louis Sabin

"Dogs are not our whole life, but they make our lives whole."

—Anonymous

L ife goes on. Our pet is gone and buried and we have done our necessary grief work. Now we can look forward to a new future and wonder if a new pet fits in the picture. Some people will feel sure they are done with walking the dog. They feel enriched by the life of their pets, but can't find space for a new pet chapter in their lives. Others jump almost immediately into a new pet's life and we can only hope they have grieved enough. In my case, I never really had a pet all to myself. They were always dogs from family and friends and neighbors. I told how important "rent-a-dogs" were in my life. So I can take the time and ask the great questions: "Will I get a dog?" "Why would I get a dog?" "What does having a dog mean in this phase of my life?"

It is not just for me to decide. My husband is not in favor of getting a dog. So he is my favorite wall of denial to bounce off all my dreams of having a dog. He forces me to dive deeper into my wish for a dog. Does my inner child long for a new pet as a final step of healing the grief? Is that healthy? I still have a way to go to convince my partner. I think he is a bit afraid of a looming "triangle."

I have had very strong feelings for the dogs in my life and they have always returned the favor. In the streets and in the parks I constantly run into my favorite Boston Terriers. Are they calling me? Or am I in danger of disillusion when I try to repeat a life's experience? So many questions to answer and decisions to be made if my husband rolls over one his one and we do get a dog.

Waking Dreams

This book is, as it stands, a waking dream in honor of Mitzie's memory. If you look at an everyday experience as if it were a dream, a waking dream, it may make it easier for you to open yourself up to a deeper meaning behind seemingly random events. Waking dreams are the surreal moments when inner visuals suddenly become vividly real and feelings become ethereal.[8] Years ago, I first read about this concept while sitting in the sun on a perfect, warm October Sunday and proceeded immediately to take the first nap I had taken in months! I woke refreshed. While I was in the midst of editing this book, I wasn't remembering many of my dreams, which is a bit unusual for me. But then I started thinking about my writing as if it were a waking dream and suddenly my dreams started to flow—or I just got motivated to grab my penlight in the middle of the night to write them down again!

If I look at my series of Mitzie dreams and this whole book as if they were waking dreams—life experiences that I believe to be real—they actually reveal an inner state of consciousness. All my dreams, sleeping *and* waking, have been helping me grieve and move on from Mitzie, a necessary precursor if I were to get a dog in my life. It says something about a longing, a yearning for childhood nostalgia, loss and thoughts about what happens when we die. If one has a belief in heaven being a good place where one is free from cares and worries, heaven is home. Who wouldn't look forward to going home again someday? I hasten to say "someday." I'm not ready yet!

All the dogs in my dreams are a part of me. Loss that's not only mine but that of my ancestral lineage is a part of what I'm writing about, too. "Heal loss through a dog's love" is a theme in my waking dreams. Mitzie and all of the part-time dogs in my dreams and reverie represent small parts of myself. The dying dogs are me facing mortality and the fear of death on one hand and seeing glimpses of the heavens and the luminous through it on the other. Seeing strength in Brewster is my inner strength calling to remind me of my "can-do" attitude. All the dogs that rise to greet the day with boundless joy are a part of me, too—not all the time, of course! I do like to sleep in! My lazy part can happily doze in the sun like Mitzie.

All those walks with Mitzie and my part-time dogs are me, too. The part of me that goes for a walk, loving it every step of the way like dogs do, is the part that feels much better only after I've taken the walk. But I don't like getting wet in a cold rain! The dogs might love it, but I don't. That is where I am different from dogs. Thank goodness! Let me count the ways. They have four legs; I have two. They have hair all over their bodies; luckily, my skin is soft and smooth. Their breath smells bad and mine better because I brush and floss. Some dogs do get their teeth brushed; that seems to be a new trend. Did Mitzie have her teeth brushed? No way. And flossed, impossible! And her breath did smell bad, too! That's why my husband doesn't mind at all to kiss me, but is disgusted when he sees a dog lick somebody's face. You see, that's where I am different! But also, we are not only different from our furry friends but, from other humans as well.

I sometimes play a game with myself after working with a client, "This is how I am different." It is meant to create healthy boundaries between therapist and client and it helps minimize the transference and counter-transference process. What is counter-transference? It is a transference that sometimes happens when a repressed part of a therapist or some buried emotion is awakened because the therapist is identifying with the experience of the client. For example, when a client comes in and shows me a picture of his or her new puppy and how much fun it is to play with him, I may feel jealous. That is a signal to me that I need to work on where that is coming from and to realize I don't have to feel jealous. I can find a way to have dogs in my life too. When counter-transference happens, a therapist really needs to be aware and work with it outside of the session either on his or her own or with the help of a mentor. The client hour is about the customer, not the unfinished business of the therapist. In some brands of therapy, it's a whole art to work with transference and counter-transference.

I have learned a lot from dogs dead and alive about being a therapist. At times, it feels like more than what I learned at Saybrook Graduate School. But what I did learn a lot about at Saybrook was working with dreams. It helps to reflect on our dreams. I had the privilege of sitting in on master dream professor, Dr. Stanley Krippner's "As If It Were My Dream" breakfast table. A student shared a dream on paper and we all analyzed it "as if it were my dream." We were doing what's called "projection" —projecting ourselves into the dream as if it were our own.

One student, Felicia, had a dream about being at an old drug store when she was a child. We talked about what the dream would mean by looking at what those stores signified to us in our childhoods. The funny thing was Felicia's last name happened to be "Walgreen" as in the famous drugstore. It was clearly written on her nametag, but none of us saw it except for Dr. Krippner himself. He viewed the drugstore as a representation of Felicia herself. Dreams can be thought of as a form of an illusion, after all, so it's easy to get lost in their interpretations!

By the way, dogs dream, too! I watched Mitzie during many a nap, shudder, yelp, huff, or whimper. I couldn't ask her what she was dreaming about. Maybe it was a nightmare about the time I pulled her tail or forced her to go through that fake wedding with Buffy next door. I'm sure she thought, *"What do they see in him for me, anyway? And that veil and flower thing they put on my head. Really, was that necessary? The things I put up with as your friend and playmate just to show you I love you unconditionally!"*

While editing certain passages of my writing I think to myself, *There I go again. Another bucket of tears.* It has been cathartic to write this book. I hope I can serve others who are going through similar emotions after losing a pet. Perhaps it will help them decide if they want to get another dog or if something else is needed to help heal the loss or fill the void. As a matter of speaking, I felt Mitzie was speaking to me through my dreams, or maybe it was a part of me and my inner child speaking, that I needed to let Mitzie go. What's revealing is that I didn't even realize before my first dream how much I was still holding on to her somewhere deep inside.

My dreams led the way. I dreamed that I needed to bury her brush in our backyard and Brewster helped me do it. The deer showed me that I wasn't alone in my parting ritual. One day I woke up smiling at realizing how much Mitzie and Oreo had embodied all of Carl Rogers' principles of empathy, genuineness and unconditional regard.

All my Mitzie dreams can be seen as individuation dreams, according to Jung's psychology. Individuation is the act of becoming whole and growing up. It resolves any triggers or conflicts transitioning from pre-teen to adulthood. Jung thought this wasn't complete until middle age. Whew, I had forgotten he said that part about middle age. And my husband warns me, it only starts seriously then! This Mitzie dream stuff has been about individuating from child to adult, and I had these dog dreams when I was in my late thirties to mid-forties, so that's normal. Furthermore, this process of awakening the inner child through the individuation process goes on until the end of life. When Jung was in the last years of his life, he went to his retreat in Switzerland and played with blocks like a child. He built a whole castle tower and played with blocks, reawakening his inner child. The power of naming this whole Mitzie business as part of an individuation process has dispelled my fears of not being normal!

I liken it to being back in my first "abnormal psychology" class in my late twenties (which was, by the way, the first time in my life I had ever taken a psychology course). There I learned all about the many disorders. Of course, upon reading about them, I wondered which rang true for me. Then I read in the textbook that every student naturally thinks he or she has a piece of them all! And the professor made jokes about it and I suddenly felt normal again.

Inner Child

If this whole book were a waking dream, it says something about my inner child and a family grieving through the loss of a dog. When looking at my inner child, I can see how it is alive in my paternal and maternal ancestral lineage. My parents were part of it, losing their parents early and growing up in the Depression. Further up the line, they were first- and second-generation immigrants who had hard times from the loss of a homeland. Maybe they never truly felt at home in the new land? The book also says something about a longing to add an addition to my family, a pet.

What does this dog book say about me? It says I'm still a child at heart. One could hope that we all are. It tells me my inner child is busy playing and processing in my unconscious. And maybe my inner child will always be connected with my memory of Mitzie. The dream, *"Burying her Brush"* in part II with the brush and deer, clearly indicated to me it was time to lay Mitzie to rest. This book, of course, is part of the journey of honoring life, death and rebirth. I feel my dreams were a call for me to write this book for my inner child. It's been therapeutic and I hope my readers will find healing in my stories or from their own memories that come up while reading. I wrote this book for my own healing and inner child and I did it sitting, so I didn't have to lie down on a couch for analysis! But you might think that my outpouring of grief about Mitzie is over the top. Then again you might have some grief hidden inside yourself. And that is what I would like to see out into the open as a result of me sharing my story, so we can share in a way our grief.

Over the years, working with archetypes that I refer to as inner characters in myself and others, I've gathered four inner-child traits that I invite others to explore in my consulting room. We all have these archetypes to some extent.

1. The Inner Child: The you growing up in your childhood.

2. The Universal Child: The you connected to heaven and earth.

3. The Orphan: The you who feels alone or who doesn't belong.

4. The Innocent: The you who is fresh, wide-eyed and curious.

Our universal child is especially the gateway to our connection with the divine. Mitzie is a clear link to my universal child and, in that way, she also brings a path to heaven and spirituality right to my door. Being closer to earth and heaven through instincts, dogs show us glimpses of other worlds. That is why Brewster was saying in my dream that he got something "spiritual" from us. I was getting something spiritual from being around him. He linked me closer to the divine above and in a way was creating a pathway to someday go home myself.

Fourth Mitzie Dream

Our dreams of beloved pets can come out of the blue, as mine did so many years after Mitzie's death, and bring comfort. The first dream of *"Mitzie in the forest"* brought Mitzie in a way back here in my present life in the Pacific Northwest, so we could work together in close quarters. The second dream, *"Burying her Brush,"* helped me put her remembrance to rest with the aid of deer imagery and Brewster. My third dream *"Just One More Walk around the Block,"* is my favorite. It felt like a closure and still stands vividly in my memory. My fourth Mitzie dream I've called *"Visiting My Parents and a Boston in Heaven."* I had this dream after hearing the fabulous authors Sue Monk Kidd, who wrote *The Secret Life of Bees*, and her daughter share stories at a talk for their upcoming book, *Traveling with Pomegranates: A Mother-Daughter Story*, about their trip to Greece. Early the next morning, I had the following beautiful dream.

I go to another home with my family, and my mom has this sweet, cute, warm, little brindle Boston Terrier in the kitchen. It's not Mitzie but a dog with a little different face and coloring. Relatives have mailed the dog to Mom saying that if she doesn't want it, she can mail it back at any time, no pressure. Till now, my parents liked that they could come and go without worrying about having a dog. A week earlier, I had told them that they might want to get another dog. Now they have one.

They use Mitzie's original orange bed and an old shoebox to make up a part of the new Boston Terrier's bed. I am crying as I hold her. It's precious and my mom is so happy again. The dog won't stop licking my hand as I sit with my whole family. We all love it and we're so happy.

It's a beautiful, sunny day. It's Mom's dog and it looks different than Mitzie because it has a smaller build and a cute, rounder, heart-shaped face. The face reminds me of Valentine candy. I can see my parents' old hot tub out the window with orange flowers all around it, but the flowers are tilted out at a strange angle, circling the hot tub and making me feel as if I'm in a strange movie.

I flash to a new scene and I see my wedding dress and remember the happiness of the day. How perfect the day was with the sunshine, calm waters, and mostly the joy of having those we love surround us in our wedding boat. Other dresses in white with speckles on them are all lined up in a row. In another scene I see my relatives, but I look at their backs while they are waiting to greet the sky full of pillows of white clouds. In the distance is a Holland America cruise boat; a synchronistic sign because my husband is Dutch. It's glorious.

Then its six years earlier, and I'm upbeat, going home again to the Southwest where my parents live, but which is in my dream my childhood home (in reality, it was in the Midwest). It is all new, bright, open, and spacious. It has high ceilings, new furniture, and everything is sparkling clean. My parents really like it there. The dog curls up in a ball, creating a sweet, loving atmosphere. It is warm and I hear laughter and feel happy to be home. Mom is warm and motherly. My parents are thrilled to have a dog again.

That is the end of the dream. It almost feels like three dreams.

In real life, a synchronicity occurs a few weeks later when I go to my own therapy session and share my puppy dream. On the way home, I stop at a shopping mall I've never been to and go to a fabric store to pick up some fleece and—what do you know? There's a pet store next door. As I walk past, I see a Boston Terrier come toward me. Upon closer look, I see that it is a brindle Boston, just like in my dream. Boston Terriers are usually black and white, and it is really unusual to see a brindle one. I stop and talk with the owner, who says it is her son's dog. I feel as if our childhood dog is smiling down upon me.

I always feel like our family, whether literal or through marriage or adoption, is our true home here on earth. If you've read John Steinbeck's book *To a God Unknown,* you might think differently about the concept of home and roots. John, the main character, had a love affair so much with the land of the Monterey Valley in California during a drought that he sacrificed himself as a kind of renewal, much like Moses did in the Bible. For him the ties to the land were as strong as family ties. Land forms deep ties within as do pets that, like the land, can ground us in our everyday life.

Interestingly, the dream didn't make me want to get a Boston Terrier. Rather, it made me feel even more of a sense of completion about the breed. It gave me a sense of peace and joy. It is as if, through the dream, my family has moved on from Mitzie and found joy in having another dog. I would venture to say it has something to do with love between mother and dog, parent and child, and love within the family.

Dreaming of Dogs—Again

When I look back at my life spending time with our family dog, rent-a-dogs and part-time pets, I see how lucky and blessed I have been to have had pets in my life. When Mitzie died my parents made a decision not to get another dog. I had allergies to both cats and dogs, but I think my parents also wanted to be able to travel more, and my grandparents had died, so trips to visit them weren't going to be the only way we spent vacations any more. Then I was in high school, college, more college, work and life as a single. I shared apartments where we had to agree to let in a pet. We're not alone in our decision about whether to bring a pet into a home. Then I started to live alone and was back in school, so again having a dog wasn't practical. Later, I had to decide if I would have one or not. I didn't.

Then I met my partner and as a couple we traveled a lot, enjoying each other. The dream came up again about having a dog and, again, I can't decide alone. I have got another roommate, a husband! In some way, I like to think I wrote this book to convince him that we need to get a dog.

But it was my dreams that led me to see I needed to heal and grieve from the loss of Mitzie. Death happens, dogs die, everyone dies in the end. Maybe I wasn't sure about getting another dog because I needed to fully grieve the first one. As I mentioned earlier, staying with Maddie, the Maltese dying in the street was hard, and she wasn't even my dog! If we choose to add a dog chapter to our lives, I know I will have to say goodbye again someday. But isn't that just part of the cycle of life and death? Isn't it better to have loved a pet than to have never loved one at all? Moving on between this pet and the next is still a question mark for us. It could be full-time, part-time or rent-a-dog time, the choice is up to us.

The memories of Part I flowed out of my pen effortlessly and the buried bones of Part II were revealed a few days later. Part III, though, became tricky because, of course, I wanted a dog and my husband wasn't immediately crazy about that idea so we came up with another plan of doing a survey on my website www. lifedeathdog.com to ask others what they thought we should do. Now, he thinks this choice should not be up to a democratic vote.

I'm torn because my husband and I like to travel and having a pet would limit our freedom to roam, in addition one might wonder whether it would be fair for the dog to be "home alone" so much. My husband isn't keen on the idea of the new, unconditional commitment it entails. He feels it's like a having a new kid on the block. And I know from experience that life with a dog is complicated. It is a responsibility that involves training and time. Maybe I or we haven't gotten a dog yet because I never fully grieved the loss of our family dog Mitzie.

Every so often I read a biography that goes something like this: "So and so lives happily with her husband and three dogs in Kalamazoo, Michigan," and I get a little jealous. I think, "Why can't I have that, too?" I have the husband part, but what about the "living with the dog" part? If it's a sunny place, I'm even more jealous because I live in Seattle where it's overcast and rains a lot!

It's taken me quite some time to get over Mitzie. I always thought I would get another dog someday, but moving, traveling, and other life pursuits always seemed to get in front of this dog dream. Since wondering if a doggie in the window is really for us, I've had some experiences that have made me question whether we're up for getting one.

Notice how I said "we," not "I," get a dog. First of all, like I said already there is the husband who really doesn't want a dog. Second, I know I would have to say goodbye again someday to a beloved pet and that would be hard all over again. And as I've mentioned, it was just as hard to say goodbye to some dear part-time dogs, too.

Many years ago, there was a sitcom I never watched, called *Married with Children*. But the new sitcom of my life, *Married with Dog*, still has to be written. And there are all the big decisions to make if—and that is a big if—we ever do get a dog. Mitzie, Oreo, Brewster, and the whole cast of master therapists are now on the other side, safe and sound. I've grieved them and then some for my ancestors and the whole collective dog soul. Let's say that my husband has a change of heart. He "rolls over" and agrees to get a dog. Now that would be some trick! He may find he's not number one in the house anymore. Then what? Or it might work the other way. If we got a dog, it could end up being more his dog than mine. I believe this because of our bonding experience with Brewster and watching dogs attach themselves to him.

Just as there are pros and cons to having a pet as part of the therapeutic encounter, there are pros and cons to not just whether we get a dog but the other decisions in the process, too, such as what kind of breed should we get? If we got another Boston Terrier, the memories of Mitzie might be too deep for me. And what about my old allergies? Do we need a presidential hypoallergergenic dog like Bo?

Should we get a puppy or a rescue dog? How about a pre-trained dog? Should it be male or female? If we do get a dog, there is no guarantee it won't bite, which is a huge responsibility. How about getting a combo: cat and a dog? Another question I would ask myself is whether I would like to have a dog as an intrinsic part of my psychotherapy practice. Should it be a therapy dog and work in my office?

But for now, it is only a dream.

Is a Dog Man's Best Friend?

I have only mentioned out loud a few times that "We might be getting a dog." Of course, I do this only when my husband is not around! When I have talked about the idea with friends, they've told me how much they think getting a dog would be great for my husband. And many, in fact, say the dog will probably end up being more his dog than our dog.

The other day, a woman told me a story similar to mine. A friend she knows has always wanted a dog and the husband really couldn't care less. Once they got the dog, something changed. The dog became her husband's. "You have to watch out for that," she said to me.

Yeah, I can totally see that one coming.

Pedro, the poodle

I'm the one who really has been yearning for a dog but, at the end of the day, who will be its best buddy? Some little voice inside me said, "Just watch. That is what is going to happen. It will end up being more my husband's dog than mine!" I already can see the dog following him around in the yard. They will be inseparable. If I happen to be outside without my husband, the dog will follow me, but the moment the man of the house steps into the yard, I will be chopped liver and the dog will be following him around. Wait a minute! Do dogs like chopped liver? Whose dog is it? Doesn't it matter who feeds the dog? Maybe I won't rate second, after all.

As I've mentioned, Brewster followed my husband around in the yard. Maybe Brewster was just following the path made by our neighbor who was always outside working with Brewster right beside him. So that was what he was comfortable with and used to following the man of the house around. Those guys do need to stick together. There is a lot of work to do and if a dog helps get that honey-do list done, more power to having a dog!

My husband's sister had a poodle, Pedro, for seven of his pre-teen and later years. My husband didn't consider it his dog, but more like his sister's and mother's dog. Dogs just love my husband, nevertheless; he seems to be kind of nonchalant about having them around.

When we go to the chiropractor, Pepper, a hypo-allergenic dog, sometimes is there to greet us. Even if the waiting room is full of dog lovers like me, she gravitates to my husband. He gives her a quick pet and Pepper happily sits right under his chair. He always finds this amusing. I tell him that I can understand how the ladies would naturally flock to him. At this comment, I usually get an eye roll.

Mitzie was really Mom's dog—I assumed, in part, because she fed her, but they really spent the most time together. And it was more my mom's dream to get another Boston like Mickey, my mom's childhood rent-a-dog, than it was my dad's dream, although he is a great dog lover, too. Oreo was more my brother-in-law's dog in some ways, because Oreo was male and the guys got to stick together in a household. It was like the men of the house bonded together working in the garage, camping, biking and playing in the yard. So this is a serious consideration when choosing a dog gender. If we choose a male dog, is it more likely to be my husband's dog than mine? Probably, but as I said, dogs gravitate so much to him that I doubt it is going to matter what gender it is. On the other hand, there are some really strong reasons other than my husband's contradiction about why not to get a dog, one of which is coyotes.

Coyotes roam our neighborhood and have snatched many a dog. The pack will be waiting in the woods while a lone coyote will taunt a dog and try to get it to follow into the woods. In spite of electric fences it isn't easy for a dog to not take the bait. I don't think I could handle it if I had a dog, large or small, that was lost to the coyotes. Bears also roam every fall, foraging to gain their thirty pounds before hibernating for the winter. But bears are mostly vegetarians so I won't be so concerned about them.

A dog is a lot of work and needs a lot of training. We can't always control what a dog is going to do. We must consider that when taking one on as part of the family. On the other hand, a dog can lighten up the house and keep hearts open. Sometimes that third presence in the form of a pet—if it isn't being used as a decoy—can make a home much more cozy and warm. Dogs bring joy and light-heartedness into a home. They make you laugh and lighten your load. Energy in a home can become stagnant and dogs keep it moving. For me, a dog's joys, benefits, and good days easily tip the scales. I can't tell you how many times I've gone into a store and my day was transformed for the better by a store owner's dog coming to greet me at the door. It's the same when I go to a family or friend's home for some lap-dog time. On top of that, pets can also help relieve the aches and pains we feel in our body.

Can your pet heal? Are the emotions animals feel any different from our own as humans? We all have heard stories of the healing power of animals. Pets have been known to carry the health issues of their owners. People who are close to their pets often have the same physical ailments as their animal. Some animals take on the physical maladies of their caregivers in an attempt to ease the suffering of their owners.

Both of Pepper's owners had issues with their right legs and, sure enough, Pepper started having issues with her right leg. It's hard to watch when your pet feels your pain. An animal psychic told Pepper's owners their dog was mimicking their symptoms because she was trying to protect them. They were to look Pepper in the eye and tell her, "You can't protect us anymore. It's not your job to protect us. It is your job to wag your tail and be happy every morning." Pepper stopped carrying their pain and walking normally within a week. What a magical way to communicate with your pet. She might, in reality, not understand your words literally, but she can apparently recognize the telepathic or emotional meaning behind them.

Sometimes I ask myself, do I want to put a dog through our psychosomatic aches and pains? That's another consideration when getting a dog. It can be a lot for a dog. Brewster possibly took on some of the hip and back pain of his owner. Oreo mimicked some health problems in sync with his owner, too. Dogs are like psychic sponges when it comes to wanting to ease the discomfort of their owners. Because of your pets, tendency to take on your pain, it is important to have boundaries with your pet and tell them to take care of themselves first.

That same thing can happen for therapists if they don't take good care of themselves. It is known as compassion fatigue. It is common among individuals who work directly with trauma victims such as nurses, psychologists, and first responders. It was first diagnosed in nurses in the 1950s. Sufferers can exhibit several symptoms including hopelessness, a decrease in experiences of pleasure, and stress symptoms. Day in, day out, functioning in caregiving environments that constantly present heart-wrenching, emotional challenges can be demanding.

Dogs can be more than a friend. They can be a protective companion to distract burglars. To be a ferocious, serious threat it has to be a large dog, preferably a German Shepherd or a Mastiff. Mitzie was too friendly and too small to scare anyone away! Protective dogs have to be fierce and attack on command. Just because a dog is large, doesn't mean it can protect a home or its master. Ironically, instead of the dog being a protector, things can go the other way. Burglars can be after the pet, too, because of its monetary value. English bulldogs, for instance, are expensive pets and valuable. When I was growing up, a neighbor's home was robbed and they feared the burglars had taken the dog.

Elwood was a beautiful Weimaraner, a breed known for its protective drive; however, Elwood had obviously been scared and had run out of the house when the burglars opened the front door. The dog was lost for a while and turned up at a neighbor's, only later that day. Meanwhile the house had been thoroughly stripped. This dog wasn't a barker so it would not have been a deterrent, anyway.

Regardless, a large dog could have a more formidable presence than a small one. It could be a protective influence, even a guard dog. Have you ever been around a protective dog? They really mean business when it comes to defending those they love. I once took a friend's three-year-old son and dog for a walk around their neighborhood. This dog was so protective of the little boy, it would literally snap at any dog that came to close to us. Really, most dogs can act as a mighty protective companion!

And let's not forget that dogs consider you one of their pack, which brings a protective presence to the home. A companion and fierce protector can be wrapped up in one package with a protection dog. Oreo was protective of those in his home. Not to literally compare dogs with people here as you would compare apples to oranges, but both pets and people have a protective presence. When I met my husband, I felt that same steady, guarded essence I had with Oreo and "protective" dogs. Early on, during an unexpected wave of grief, I experienced again what it was like to be in the presence of a rock and, like Oreo, be with someone who stood guard like a regal prince throughout the meltdown. There is no trying to figure it out; he just stands by, doesn't say anything unless I prompt a response, will hold me as long as it takes, and just allows me to let it all hang out. That is a gift, for sure. Because Oreo was a protective, male pseudo-guard dog and had similar traits to a protective man, it was wonderful to have this guarding presence around. There is something to be said for a constant, strong dog or human being by one's side to balance out the feminine yin within.

Can we even begin to imagine what all this transference, mimicking and guarding means for the dog in the house? Life as a dog must be hard this way, sometimes. Or maybe they just love the hard life. Then, they really must be our best friends!

Reality and Relationship

Every relationship has chapters and turning points, and the longer the relationship the more chapters it contains. Do we need a dog chapter in our lives? How would having a dog chapter affect our relationship? How can I even be looking at a potential rebirth and dreaming about dog breeds if we haven't been able to agree upon it as a couple? It would have to be "our" decision. It can be a difficult discussion in a family because each person has different needs and thoughts about getting a pet. It could be seen as easier to bring a dog into a family if the couple already had the responsibility for a child, for instance. A friend got a Labrador much to her husband's discontent. He agreed but said it would be her responsibility. "Sure enough he meant it, when the dog has diarrhea I am the one cleaning it up."

Another friend told me about my husband, "He wants a dog. He just doesn't know it, yet." That kind of thinking could get me into trouble. I hate to admit it, but I was watching "Keeping up with the Kardashians" to see what the fuss was about. It was depressing, to say the least. The mother, Kris, had gone behind the father's, Bruce Jenner's, back and wishes and brought home puppies for their youngest daughters. It was a manipulative, controlling move, for sure. Not talking through such a decision is so wrong. A girlfriend once suggested the same thing to me: "Just get the dog and bring it home. He'll learn to love it." I don't think that would go over well at all. My husband asked me what in the world I was watching and I told him about Kris's dark mother move. He said, "If you ever just

came home with a dog, that would be it. I would be gone."
I think he meant it, too.

I don't dare joke about it. But my husband does, apparently feeling free to do it. He would have loved to play a dog in *Saturday Night Live*.

"I should have known before I proposed! I could have asked you, 'Do you want a ring or a collar?'"

"Both," I would have quickly and happily replied.

"I didn't know that. Now, you have a ring, but you have *me* on a leash, too. Do you think you please me when you call me a dog with tears? If you keep comparing me with a dog, let's reverse evolution. A third of Americans doesn't believe in it anyway. So let's elevate the dog in the pecking order of evolution and place it above the human being."

It seems he has learned to become a good American, because his remarks taste like my sarcasm, sometimes. If he would read this, he could maybe lightly joke about being compared to a dog, or he could see it as a reversal of fortune, nearly an insult and showing "I am not enough anymore."

In the past, he teased me often, referring to himself as number two in the house when we cared for our neighbor's dog. "Brewster is number one," he would say with a hint of playful jealousy. Brewster got lots of attention from me, as I've related. In my view, comparing Oreo, Mitzie, and other dogs I've loved to the healing presence of a man is a great compliment, to the dogs. But my husband likes to say, "Husbands come second to children and dogs."

He is done with being a caregiver. He has raised four kids and thinks that's enough. He has done his duty. His kids are grown and gone. He regrets not seeing his children and grandchildren more often, they live thousands of miles away, but, on the other hand, seeing them every day would be too much. He wants to enjoy his retirement without daily duties. So he feels strongly about no-dog-care.

Marriage is about negotiating, sharing goals and each other's happiness. He is the steward of my happiness as I am his. My husband resents the whole idea of getting a dog if it means he would be put upon with responsibilities to care for it. He would feel imposed upon if I got a dog and expected him to play a large role in caring for it. Somebody has to put water in the dog dish and he doesn't want it to fall always on him. I would have to love and respect his needs and not play the guilt card. For instance, I would have to walk the dog ungrudgingly without his help. Then we are where we should be. The man wears the ring, the dog wears the collar. It's easier to put a leash on a collar than a ring on a finger, that's for sure!

I get it that one of the reasons my husband is reluctant to get a dog is because he is the alpha in the house and the dog will know it. So discipline could fall to him. He'd make sure the dog is treated as a dog, not as a little human. We seem to agree on that topic. His no-dog-care stance is only fair in theory and in practice highly unrealistic. We need to come up with a compromise that will center on caring for each other's needs. Not on the care of the would-be pet, but prioritizing care for ourselves.

We do agree on one point about dogs in general. Dogs don't belong in our bedroom. For me, this goes back to my association with allergies. So I am not really a fan of sharing my bed with a dog. Or, imagine, dogs! But, a couple of years ago, my husband was laid up in bed with a broken foot and, a while later, it was my turn with a severely sprained ankle. I wonder, if we had had a dog at those times, would we have stuck with our imaginary rules? I told you, dogs have amazing healing powers. I'm convinced their attention could have helped both of us heal our right foot quicker and better. Of course, they couldn't have been stepping in and driving our car. That's where you need a loving spouse!

What do you think? Do we need a couples' therapist to solve our dilemma? Too bad we can't turn it around and get a dog first. In my opinion, a dog could easily take the place of a couples' therapist should we ever decide we need one. Claudia, who I introduced you to in Part I was a natural couples' therapist. Similarly, I knew a couple who would talk to their dog Fido, instead of to each other whenever they had a disagreement. All three of them would be in a room, creating a triangle: husband, wife, and dog. Jung says there is tension between the two until the third appears. In this case, the third is not a child but a dog. When the dog died, they really had a hard time communicating with each other because they were so used to telling Fido, "Tell your dad (mom) that he (she) needs to do so and so," instead of saying it directly to the spouse. That was an unhealthy triangle, of course. I can't imagine such a world! Nevertheless, Fido should have been charging bones by the hour for the work he did!

I haven't given much thought about what I want to do in retirement. I think that as long as I can sit in a chair, listen and help, I want to keep working. If I don't get a dog before too long, at least I am comforted with the idea that I can look forward to getting a therapy dog maybe in retirement. It would be fun to take a therapy dog around in the community where a little pet "TLC" may be in order. I like the idea of pet therapy and think in the right circumstances it would enhance my work. But whether my husband and I get a dog before I retire is our joined decision. And there are so many questions to consider. It still is the big "If."

For Better and for Worse

Now and again as a therapist I'm moved because I see women coming to me who are in deep pain and feel emotionally alone in their relationships. They say: "My husband isn't very emotional," or "He gets uncomfortable when I cry," or "My partner isn't like me." Often, guys don't know how to sit with their women while they lose it. Men want to fix everything. Or tell the wife to snap out of it. "Why can't you just be happy? Can't you see that we're OK?" Men often feel helpless. They don't get it. Some men don't have the inner reservoir to be moved, to know it's safe to let emotions come tumbling out. They never learned or saw a wide range of emotional sentiments modeled in their early years. Brain scans have shown that men's brains do not react in the same way as women do to the sound of a distressed baby. We are physiologically wired differently. Men may not realize what women want.

And what do they want in life? Isn't that like a Holy Grail question? Let me give you my short version of a story of Gawain, King Arthur's nephew and a great champion for women. Be sure to look this old story up online, for its clue is as fresh today as it was yesterday.

To save his king, the gallant Gawain has agreed to marry an ugly hag who promised the king the answer to the question "What do women want in life?" The answer will free the king from a fight with an invincible knight. On the wedding day the hag gives Arthur the promised answer, but, faithfully, Gawain sticks to his promise to marry her. After the wedding, in the nuptial bedroom when Gawain turns around to face his duty, the spell is broken and the hag suddenly turns into a beautiful bride. Gawain is excited, of course, to have such beauty at hand, but his wife warns him: "I can only be beautiful for half of each day. Either you can be proud to show me at court during the day, or you enjoy my delight in the privacy of our bed at night. What is your choice?"

Gawain has to think for quite a while. He feels tormented. Each choice is delightful and bitter at the same time. Finally, when he gives up, he sees the light. "Lady, it is not for me to choose. It is your choice. Tell me what it will be." His bride jumps into his arms, the spell is now completely broken and she is now beautiful day and night. And they live happily forever after. This was the answer all along: women want sovereignty to live their own lives and make their own choices. Then they can choose to share whatever they have, too.

Vintage Boston

According to this Arthurian legend, women want free choice in sovereignty, but they also want a safe place to go and be listened to when they need emotional support. If a man can't give that, dogs may provide that unspoken empathy, tenderness and unconditional love that women often need in times of support. As I've shared from experience, they bring a unique brand of empathy to a human crying jag. Dogs don't have those deeper questions we have as humans, so some dogs can just be with tears. Also, those balls of fur don't talk back which means unquestionable acceptance.

Do men get it that this is one of the fundamental ways women are asking them to be present? Women often want to feel connected to their men while they are being all things feminine. The feminine element of being able to be really present with what is alive in ourselves as women, our inner voices, emotions, creativity, receptiveness. As women, we may want to give as well as receive, feel an inner softness, femininity, and vulnerability.

The focus of the relationship can't always be about supporting the woman emotionally, either. If there isn't space in the relationship for the man to process his struggles, pains, and sorrows, the couple is in trouble. It's unbalanced if one foot is always crying over the other. Dan Rather, who is in touch with his inner feminine side and has been known to cry in public, said about crying, "[It's] genuine. It's authentic. We live in a society where authenticity is very hard to come by."[9]

Can guys grieve in today's society? Many have heard about the studies that show that little boys are groomed to fight, not cry. They stick up their hands in the air more often to ask questions in class, showing assertiveness to start with. But many of the traditional traits and roles of men and women are changing. Do grown men have the emotional maturity to stand by their woman? It probably depends on experience. Did they have to dive down into their own emotional reservoirs enough to be able to be present for a woman during her dives? We hear of women "standing by their man," and the lyrics to the song, "Stand by Your Man" might come to mind, but support goes both ways. I don't think I've heard of song lyrics like, "Stand by your woman when she cries a river dry."

Times are changing; the inner characters or archetypes that symbolize what it means to be a man or a woman are in flux as they have been since the beginning of time. In ancient Egypt, the yin and yang polarities were reversed. Nut was the great Goddess of the sky, while Geb, the great God, lay on earth under her. Just like doomsayers talk about a massive earth pole shift coming between the North and South Poles, perhaps we are headed for yet another yin and yang switch. Because of the 2008 economic downturn, many men, unfortunately, lost their jobs. As a result, many women have had to go back to work (earning, by the way, only eighty cents for every dollar a man makes). The men have had to pick up household duties at home. They are taking care of the kids or finding themselves making dinner because their wife is commuting long hours to and from work. This is a challenge in many households. Where it all leads to, we don't know yet. Women are juggling a lot of family relational and work-related roles. Women often are competing in and for jobs and finding that the whole patriarchal system is wearing them out. Recovering the feminine and balancing it within the masculine is part of what the changing times are about.

What I do know is that women will keep on crying because we come from the water element. Our energy is like a flowing river, and we know what happens when people try to reverse the flow of a real river. We end up with a mess, like flooding the land. And we can't stop Mother Nature. Recent world events like the earthquakes and tsunamis have proved that. The oceans are rising. Rivers, like the Mississippi, are widening and Mother Nature has a mind of her own. She flows wherever she goes and little can be done to stop her. On the other hand, we also know the highest state of water is divine love. And we as women are all about relationships, because water is how we connect to others. It is through these watery, tear-filled "meltdowns" that we come to experience those moments of unconditional love through our connections, be they animal or human, that represent divine love flowing to, in, and through us. Simply being held closely by a silent man who refuses to be drawn into words opens the floodgates.

There have been a few times, too, when my rock has lost it and cried with me. Those are very special times. That he can be so moved by my tears helps me heal in a profound way. It doesn't happen often, but when it does, it lets me know I'm not alone. Likewise, his stories have moved me to the point where I feel I would do anything for this man.

I'm learning that sometimes couples need to be able to grieve together, whether the source is one or the other's pain or their marital problems. For instance, I've seen couples break up who have suffered the loss of a child and not found a way to grieve together. A couple that grieves together stays together. Pets have a shorter life span than humans so when a couple or family has a pet that dies it teaches them about the cycle of life and death. Children often learn of grief through the death of a grandparent or a pet. Grief has a way of bringing couples and family members closer. Just grieving the loss of our neighbor's dog Brewster brought my husband and myself closer together. Having a dog to celebrate its life and honor its loss can bring a couple closer too.

Dogs with Tears

What are the roles today for a man and woman? I feel for men because they have, as I said just now, no idea what women want. That is, in some part, because women often have no clue as to what we want, let alone the ability to articulate it.

The television Learning Channel had a program in 2002 called, "Alpha Male," discussing the changing roles in our society and suggesting that we are smack in the middle of a giant gender experiment. Most of the usual ways in which men mold their roles, relate and exercise power for centuries don't work anymore. In prehistoric times, the alpha male's testosterone helped him survive and thrive. He went out hunting, brought home the kill, spread his seed and thought of himself as the leader of the pack. Eons later men (and women) have realized typical roles don't work anymore because the genders have become more equal on all levels. Balancing and equality is a good thing! Men are gradually integrating more of their inner feminine through the years; hence, we will probably have more men who are like a dog with tears. A man's sensitive supportive side can be just as good as a dog's unconditional positive regard. But the balancing act is not without growing pains on both sides, particularly for men to read women. By the way, John Wayne types are still around—the typical, iconic alpha male. The Alpha Male show interviewed men on the street asking them what women wanted. "I have no clue," was a common response. They clearly were not educated in Arthurian legend.

The show merely illustrated that men are just waiting for women to figure it out so they can respond in kind. So how are men supposed to know? Women need to realize that they have to tell men, "This is how you can support me. This is what I need you to do." Perhaps one of the ways women need to be more direct with men is telling them when they need to just listen and be the rock. Don't try to fix anything, just be. Women have to spell it out for men; otherwise, men are lost in the desert. Men are like camels that really want to drink from the well of women's love but just don't know how to find the water. Women have to be that water element which is associated with the feminine principle in many traditions. Basically, according to psychologist Carl G. Jung, we are all androgynous beings just trying to balance out our masculine and feminine sides. Alpha males have an inner feminine, too, that needs support in a partnership.

We as women have to get in touch with our emotional natures and find a way to let down our guard and cry once in a while. We were born female, not male, so tears are just a part of the deal. And speaking on behalf of women I believe we have to do our inner work: to heal, to grieve, and to lead the way so that the feminine principle itself becomes more balanced and whole. Women have to heal and learn to recognize the archetypes of the victim, martyr, offender and rescuer. All of the shadow feminine forces that live in each of woman have to be recognized and transformed.

Healing often starts with tears symbolizing the water element. When I fell down as a little kid and skinned my knee, what did my mother do first to heal it? She comforted me and washed it with water then put on some Neosporin and a bandage. Water is where it starts, that intuitive part of our subconscious mind that flows like a river. It is empathy, the emotional body. It signifies our relationships and how we connect to others.

The challenge with water is to have clear boundaries. Without boundaries, water will flow everywhere. In the fun game *Rock, Paper, Scissors*, in which two people simultaneously form one of the three shapes with an outstretched hand, rock beats scissors, paper beats rock and scissors beats paper. As a kid, I played a more balanced version that included fire and water. Water beats rock because a rock can't stop the water. It just flows around it. But what the rock can do is be there, be present with unconditional positive love while the water and tears flow.

A man becomes a woman's rock when he can withstand yet another onslaught of tears without taking it too personally, figuring it out, blaming, judging, or solving the problem. When a man realizes that he can't stop the water, it just goes around him. The rock can be there to let the water know it's not alone. He can be her ground, support, and anchor when she feels like falling apart. A man can be a rock when a woman needs to grieve and let go. Animals, who are more grounded naturally, can be a woman's support when the rock isn't around. But animal friends can't talk or offer a shoulder when a woman is crying a bucket of tears.

What does all this talk about alpha males and gender experiments have to do with dogs and being in between one pet and the next? What is a guy to do when his woman clearly states that she wants a dog, but he is afraid the dog will take over his role as family comforter? A pet can be a comfort just like a partner can. Can you have both? Does one compete with the other? Doesn't having a pet make both partner's lives a little fuller with more love and bring a bit more of those therapeutic healing principles like unconditional positive regard, empathy and genuineness into their lives? But we have to be aware of the consequences. How much transference is really going on between partners and pets?

As Joseph Campbell says, "If your marriage is not your highest priority, you're not really married."[10] That is a lot to live up to! A benefit of being married is that you have the person who vowed to love you through thick and thin. Make it work and make it last! We are constantly reminded that divine love comes in all forms: animal, human, and spiritual. But, sometimes, we as women just can't do better than the feel of a human heart beating with our tears running down his chest all the while.

My husband has tears to shed with me, but does a

dog? They may whimper and feel sad. I don't doubt that dogs have emotions, but they don't cry. At the end of the day, dogs can't talk and are from the animal—not the human—kingdom. That is why hanging out with the human kingdom is essential. A man can learn to be a comfort like a dog. Seeing men as rocks and women as the ones who cry may be old fashioned in one sense. As I mentioned, times are changing and so are gender roles. My husband is a man who can cry. He is a "dog with tears." Men are supposed to have emotions and shed a tear or two. Roles in marriage are changing, too, and one of the benefits of marriage is the support it provides.

Recently, science has discovered that dogs have the same brain structures that produce emotions in humans. Dogs also have the same hormones and undergo the same chemical changes that humans do during emotional states. Dogs even have the hormone oxytocin, which, in humans, is involved with feeling love and affection for others. With the same neurology and chemistry that people have, it seems reasonable to suggest that dogs also have emotions that are similar to ours. However, studies suggest that dogs have the emotional level of two-year-old children. Nevertheless, it is difficult for a man to be always around and present. That is easier for a dog.

There are times when someone is so moved by your pain that they cry with you. That has happened to me many times in life and it always confirmed some deeper knowing that I'm not alone. It happened with friends, of course, and on other occasions, for instance, a few, really rare times when I was in therapy. When a therapist who was working with me became moved to tears by my story, I was always surprised at first and then I felt a sense of peace knowing that somebody really got it. Those therapists got it because they truly felt my pain or it sparked a similar pain they were holding within themselves. I intuitively knew that they have felt something somehow similar in their own souls. And I felt understood at some very deep level. Not that I needed the tears. Empathy is often an unspoken presence that just is.

Here you can clearly see the difference. Psychologists talk about two types of intimacy: physical and emotional. Obviously, a pet is there to hug but isn't there to hold hands or kiss or for other sexual activity. Pets can't talk unless we reckon telepathic communication is the same as human-to-human dialogue. The healing power of touch, belonging, and love do come from those adorable bundles of fur. With beloved pets, one can create an intimate proximity of shared personal space. Their connection to the animal kingdom can bring out in us a sense of connecting to the divine grace that flows all around us. In a way, I think that is a form of true emotional intimacy.

While a dog is incredibly empathic in its nonverbal love cues and verbal ruffs, it can't say in so many words, "I've been there." Human beings allow another kind of emotional intimacy to emerge because they can say, "I've been there." That's where petting your dog isn't the same as having a human connection. What humans miss in their pet is another form of intimacy. Humans have a general desire to belong and to love, which often is satisfied within an intimate relationship. Genuine intimacy in human relationships requires dialogue, transparency, and vulnerability. Emotional intimacy typically develops after a certain level of trust has been reached and personal bonds have been established. True vulnerability then emerges. Dogs don't have the same life pains as humans, so they communicate a different kind of empathy.

On the other hand, while pets are not able to talk, don't offer sympathy and don't give their distraught owner a *boy do I pity you* look, they are wired for true empathic understanding all the way. That will work, sometimes, when we are looking for emotional intimacy and are disappointed in our human relations. Nevertheless, allowing ourselves to be open and vulnerable with another human being is part of the appeal of forming emotional bonds in the human versus animal kingdom. Animals live in a different kingdom and communicate by nonverbal means. We can understand that our pets on an emotional level empathize with us, but human beings provide connections we can't find in a pet.

"I'm a dog with tears." This is what my husband said upon reading my comparisons to dogs and humanistic therapy. Luckily, he has a sense of humor about my writing about men, life, and dogs. And he has a certain understanding of women—probably more than the average man.

Doggie Decisions

C.G. Jung coined the term *synchronicity* to describe meaningful coincidences. Synchronistic occurrences are unique and rare, not repeatable or predictable. If we are looking for a cause, we can't find one. These events can be irrational, and impersonal, but, according to psychologist Jung are required for our happiness. That's where my Bostons come in. Every once in a while, I run into a Boston, leashed or not, who can't wait to greet me. I just love days like these. On a hike, I felt a *déjà vu* kind of feeling when a dog came out of nowhere, excited to say, "Hi" to me. Lately, they have been in sets of two. I think they can sense that I'm a Boston lover. Or maybe it's my imagination, and all Bostons—no, most Boston Terrier *dogs*—are that friendly. Now it's really a special day if the dog happens to be brindle, not black and white. Then I really feel like our dog's angel wings are nearby. Is this a simple coincidence or is it a synchronicity?

I asked for a clue about moving forward with this book on one occasion. The next day I went to the beach with a girlfriend and ran into not only one but two Boston Terriers! Maybe it's my imagination again, but I think Boston owners resemble their dogs, they are some of the most friendly, down-to-earth people I ever meet. Always happy to let me pet their dog and share their love of Bostons with a former Boston owner.

If we get a dog the first and foremost question, for me, is whether we should repeat the breed and get another Boston Terrier. All things considered, do we think our family should get another one? I don't think I ever will. It would be too much of a repeat from the past. Too many memories and the whole idea of putting another animal through all the pet projections I would place on it, seems almost cruel. It would always be compared in some way to Mitzie. The dog would have a complex just from all the Boston knick-knacks it would see on the Christmas tree every year. It wouldn't be fair, somehow to the dog.

I think if I would have had a dog earlier, perhaps I would not have this unfinished mourning business and perhaps would not be writing about immortalized Mitzie. Sure, every dog has its own unique personality. Whether dogs have a soul is a worthy debate I won't indulge in at this moment. But they are each different, so if I were to get a Boston, it would have to be in another time, place, and circumstance altogether. I'm no longer the little girl who would pull on a dog's tail, either, thank goodness. Maybe if the dog was black and white and not brindle like Mitzie, it would be easier. Perhaps if the dog was male instead of female that would make a difference. No, I still think it would be best for both sides if I went with a clean, fresh new slate and got another breed altogether. Plus, Mitzie was not hypo-allergenic, something to consider with my history of being tested positive for dog allergies. The good news is that poodles *are* hypo-allergenic. We could get one of those. I hear they are smart, loyal, and affectionate. Bless Mitzie's heart. She can be the one and only special Boston Terrier in our family.

Another reason not to get a Boston is because they are so popular now. They are in commercials everywhere, probably because of their cute expressions and clean black-

Boston Ad

and-white image. They are so photogenic! It could be fun to get a dog that is different and unique from what I grew up with.

Should we get a little dog or a big dog? I've grown fond of large dogs. I never would have thought I'd like them, but I do. Brewster cured me of my large-dog prejudice. Even though my husband grew up with a poodle, he isn't partial to them. Anyway, he only likes large dogs. He doesn't understand what the attraction is with small dogs. He sees a huge difference between "pets" and "dogs." He thinks little "lap-dogs" are just "pets" or "lappies" and doesn't see the charm of having a small dog. I hardly dare to write this down! It seems he is not afraid to offend many dog owners! Brewster walked the yard with him and they were such great buddies. Maybe that confirmed his prejudice against small dogs.

Brewster surely was a large dog and he reminded me of the hound seen in pictures and sculptures of the goddess Diana. Diana, or Artemis in Greek, was the goddess of both wild and domestic animals. Her temple in Ephesus, Turkey was one of the wonders of the world. When I traveled to Ephesus, I saw Diana often portrayed with bow and arrow and accompanied either by a deer or hounds. Her hounds stand by and seem to act as her guardians and protectors. So you see, dogs have given a protective presence going back to ancient times.

If we would not get a Boston Terrier and prefer a medium to large dog what kind of dog should we get? Should we get more than one dog? Some people have the same

Diana, Ephesus, Turkey

number of members (human and pet beings combined) in the household they grew up in as they do as adults. For example, if there were three family members in the home growing up, a woman who lives alone may have two dogs to round up to three. I think it might be easier to have more than one dog because it changes the pet dynamic I grew up with, making trans-ference less likely. It might help me to have two dogs so that I would have a totally different experience with a pet or pets.

Once I heard about this household human-to-pet magic ratio, I started to hear stories that prove the subconscious can work in mysterious ways to keep that magic number in place. For instance, when our neighbor's daughter started looking at colleges in her senior year, they got a new puppy so when she left in the fall they would still be the magic number of five. They admitted they could be doing it to avoid feeling they were living in a soon-to-be empty nest.

Dogs may even be in on the collective unconscious workings of the magic ratio. When my eldest niece went away to college the number in the household shrunk from six to five. Oreo got sick shortly after she left and passed away later that following year. That left four in the household including Dash and my younger niece. A year later Dash got sick. Before he passed over, they went out and got Sophie, the puppy. So when one dog gets sick there may be a subconscious tendency to replace the household ratio. By the way, Dash wasn't wild about having a puppy join the nest. He came around after Sophie got fixed and he was feeling under the weather. Suddenly he was her big

Oreo is sad she's leaving

brother and was going to look out for her. He made sure the big dogs didn't bother her when they went to the dog park, for instance. So watch for that pattern when the oldest child in a household goes to college and see if the numbers stay the same by getting another pet. Otherwise, the reality of a shrinking household and empty nest syndrome just might sneak in.

Having a second dog also has the added advantage of relieving guilt when a dog is left alone. They would have a buddy and could keep each other company. The dog is less likely to feel abandoned when it is left and would be less reliant on human interaction. When Dash died, little Sophie was sad. She seemed to be at a loss when she accidently heard an old video of her brother and she ran around the house looking for him. If Sophie had another dog in the house, she may have transitioned better.

But, for us, the biggest advantage to having our two dogs would be that I wouldn't have to share one with a husband whom dogs seem to adore. Instead of still being without a dog I've campaigned so hard for, if we had two dogs, there would be more than enough for both of us. It might be better *feng shui* because they could help balance the yin and yang energies in the house, too! More work, perhaps. But dogs love to be in packs, so I would think they would be happier with another dog than being alone.

Of course, my husband would like to have a word, if not the last word (he always says that is for women!). He wonders how many dogs he would need to make up for a family of four children, daughters- and sons-in-law, and three grand-daughters. Why wouldn't we get a whole animal and human pack at once? Then they could take care of themselves and maybe we could have a foxhunt in the front yard!

I'll have to think awhile about my last word.

Puppies, Training, Gender and Cats

Have you ever just sat and watched dogs run at a dog park? One day, out walking by a lake with a friend, we came upon a local dog park. Dog parks by the water are the best for viewing pleasure. Watching dogs run, leap, splash, and play is pure joy, exuberance and chaos all at the same time. We watched a bully dog run after all the little dogs, some were just scared puppies. The little dog owners were frustrated. The owner of the big dog had no alpha upper-hand to rein in his behavior. Training a dog is really a lot of work and comes with great responsibility to ensure it can behave itself socially. Dogs can be like children. I think of that scene and how much work get-

Mitzie on Grandma's couch

ting a puppy would be. Mitzie was left with a babysitter when she was a puppy for an overnight. My parents returned to find the room a complete disaster. She had got into the garbage and torn the room apart. As the story goes, Mitzie must have been bored and the babysitter didn't walk her enough or pay her enough attention. It's a lot to take care of an adult dog as it is. A puppy is a handful.

I took care of Mitzie for a week when I was nine to get my dog Girl Scout patch. Feeding, washing, walking, and researching her breed was all a part of my responsibility. She was moving into her last years when I took care of her that week and I remember loving it and also knowing I had to be dependable. What if I forgot to feed her? I wanted to learn to be a professional dog-sitter!

Puppies need safe exercise, play and socialization. To escape the puppy upheavals, one option is, of course, to get a pre-trained puppy, but that would be more expensive. Another good choice is to get a mature dog rather than a puppy. That, though, has its own pros and cons.

You could

1. Inherit somebody else's behavior and training problems,

2. Have to face the chance of losing your dog sooner based on simple math,

3. Miss out on that bonding time with a puppy— they are so cute and adorable.

On the other hand, you could

1. Really be helping out a rescue or mature dog find a good home,

2. Be relieved of some of the work of training a puppy,

3. Save your furniture from being chewed, your carpet from accidents,

4. Get a more realistic picture of what you're getting with an adult dog.

Every dog's temperament is different. As I've mentioned before, not all dogs can handle tears. Cuddling doesn't always run in dog bloodlines, either, and even if they are cuddly, they don't do so equally. Oreo's brother Dash was a great choice when you needed a good cuddle but often bolted whenever tears arose. Dash didn't have quite the same unconditional positive regard traits as Oreo; he had other gifts, like his cuddly nature.

It is interesting how one brother was more yin, or girl-like, in traits and the other more yang, or boy-like, in personality, though both were boys. Because Mitzie was a girl I just assumed that female dogs would be more affectionate and cuddly. That was before meeting Oreo and Dash, a pair of male Havenese brothers. Dash, the blonde who was the less dominate of the pair was affectionate, but more finicky in some ways. Oreo who was more dominant was also surprisingly affectionate. Maybe it was his

Dash and Oreo

instinctive, protective nature making sure that everyone in their pack, the human family included, was all good. Dash acted more like a female dog than Oreo, but was less likely to recognize when someone needed a good cuddle. Female dogs are loving in their own way, but in my experience just a tad less affectionate, finicky at times. Who would have thought? Many people might beg to differ. But that has been my experience, though I'm no dog expert by any means.

I've never thought of myself as a cat person. But cats sure are easier to take care of. How would a dog and cat get along? What would be the reasons to get a combination of the two? Could they keep each other company? Maybe I should mention my husband's take here. He considers himself a cat. He is a Leo and feels a deep connection to the Big Cats—lions and tigers, black panthers and snow leopards. Once, when he saw somebody jogging on a bike path, he smiled and said "There goes a dog, panting, heart racing, tongue flapping out of his mouth. Not for me. Let me snooze and sleep in front of the stove. Then, when I wake up, I only have to stretch and am ready for action. No need to exercise, I'll jump right on the mantelpiece. By the way, I can take good care of myself, as well. Who wants to be a dog?" Does that mean we live as cat and dog?

We have stray cats in our neighborhood. There is a black one that darts in and out, trying to catch mice for us. Another cat seems to be a stray but actually belongs to a neighbor. This cat is not so popular, probably because she thinks everybody else's yard is a litter box. She is like a dog that way. We have a small herb garden, divided into nine squares outside of our front door. I have given up planting in the ninth square because this is one of her litter boxes. She sneaks in there, does her business, and then slips out before anyone notices her. I know it's this cat because other neighbors have been complaining about her practices—and I caught her lounging in the ninth square one time. Apparently, her owners do not have a litter box in the house. It reminded me of Mitzie's sunny naptime garden patch outside the house. Except Mitzie didn't do her business in her square! Either way, I love all stray and neighborly cats in my yard because that means fewer mice. But with cats you don't get all the benefits of having a dog you can walk. If I had a dog I would get more exercise because the dog needs that walk! But to be honest, I often have a pleasant walk around the lake with my husband. So much for being a cat.

Active Imagination

Each dog is different and special in its own way with its unique personality. This is evident when I am out on my neighborhood walks chatting with dog owners and getting my dog fix for the day. As I walk away, I sometimes can't help but drift into the realm of wonder. I wonder if my husband and I had a dog, would I be out walking it faithfully right now? What would it look like? Would it be spotted, blonde, brown or black? Would we be good dog owners? How would the dog cope when we traveled? How would my husband have handled having a dog if I was the one on the road? What about having a boy dog? Would it be an alpha male type, strong and willful like Oreo? Does it make a difference if it is a male or female dog?

What is the feminine anyway? Hang out with a dog and she will tell you. The more I watch dogs and the more rent-a-dogs I hang out with the more they show me a feminine way of being. Animals are connected to the mother nature's kingdom and can help keep us grounded. They don't have to wear shoes so their paws walk right on the bare ground connecting to mother earth. They feel the grass in the ground, the sand of the beach and the hot pavement in the park.

Dogs are all heart to show up at the door when you come home. They run up to greet you and lick you to let you know that you're loved. When you are depressed they cheer you up. Dogs love to cuddle and sit by your side when you cry. They are incredibly loyal and intuitive. They seem to know what's going on with you, sometimes before you even do. They are pure joy. They are so devoted, nurturing and comforting. All these are qualities of feminine energy. Dogs teach a feminine way and approach to life. But does it really make a difference whether you get a male or female dog. No, not really in my opinion both genders have a way of being there for you in the moment.

What kind of dog traits would my dog have? They say the dog ends up being an extension of the owner. How would that manifest with us? Would it be friendly? Jump on others! Make me laugh? My husband makes me smile and laugh every day with his charming wit. Would our dog do the same? Would its personality match ours in any way? What kind of mischief would it get into? If we got a puppy would it make it through obedience training? If it went to doggy day care would they give it stars on their performance board letting me know what a good doggy it was? That it socialized and played nice with other dogs, ate its food and did what it was told? Would we succeed in treating our dog as a mammal, not a human being?

At the end of the day dogs are mammals and humans are a species all of their own. Let's hope we could look at the decision to get a dog as potential pet owners, not pet parents and not treat a pet just like a person. I would have to be aware that the dog isn't filling an empty void in our relationship or unhealed grief in my inner child. I hope we would be responsible, loving pet owners. That the pet would become part of the family and remind us to play and not take life so seriously. That I could share the love and joy of having a pet with others as has been done for me over the years. That the dog would be a grounding influence in not just my life, but that it would play a role as a therapy dog in my practice having a positive influence in my clients lives as well. Whew, that is giving this should -we-get-a-dog decision some serious thought!

Could the new dog ever or would it ever surpass the memory of Mitzie? I met a dog owner the other day and, as we were talking, she said she had another dog before this one that she really missed after it died. That dog did this, that and the other thing. "It died, and I was devastated and eventually got this dog here." She was in transition, you could tell and wasn't as thrilled or deeply in love with this new dog, yet. Is it ever the same for pet owners as it was with the first dog? Maybe not. But if I remember that each dog is different and the essence of the dog brings me just what I need at that time of life, it will be the right dog for me or us.

Would it work to just visualize having a dog? My hairdresser, Sue, tells me she grew up believing and knowing she could manifest anything just through the sheer power of her intent and visualization. "My grand-mother taught me how to visualize. I grew up hearing about it every day" she tells me when I start talking about manifesting one's heart's desires. I have been using visualization techniques for years, but never thought about using them to get a dog! What if I did what Sue's grandma told her to do and just sat in a chair and thought about what I wanted to create in having a dog of our own? And how do I do that when my husband isn't really onboard with the whole idea? I'm a fan of Neville's work. He has readers visualize and really feel the manifestation in their whole body, all their senses, until it they feel it even in their bones.

Wouldn't it be fun to be able to visualize all the personality traits we would like in our pet? But who can control what traits a pet that comes into our lives will really have? Just thinking about visualizing makes me daydream back to days with Mitzie. I've heard from other Boston Terrier owners that they do love to run in circles! I don't know if this is a common personality trait of the Boston Terriers breed in general! Mitzie would run around the circumference of our entire backyard whenever she saw Mr. Heilman, our next door neighbor. Likewise, in my grown up neighborhood, Nicky, another Boston Terrier, is reported to run around the side of his house in circles. Mitzie would run around the circumference of our yard to the edge of where she was allowed whenever she saw our neighbor. He was one of the most gentle, soft spoken, caring men, taking care of an invalid wife. So I guess I can understand what all the excitement and fuss was about for Mitzie running into Mr. Heilman. He never had a bone for her, just a simple hello and a pat on the head. Joker, their dog, was around when I was a toddler, and I have faint memories of hanging out in my stroller on the Heilman's patio with Joker nearby. That trait of loving to run in circles and chase its tail around the yard would be more about the personality breed and not so much about the essence of what kind of dog we would attract into our lives.

I would like to imagine it would be a magical process. of a higher divine order to bringing the right dog into our lives. Sure, we have our intentions, essence, visualizations,

practical know-how and search that would go into it. I can dream big when it comes to getting another dog. Patricia had had a dream about a seeing a white cat on the property of their flower essence farm. And one day there it was, walking up the driveway. I just love stories like that. And what a special cat she was, as I told you. Last year, my husband's

Bruno, the rescue dog

daughter had this kind of luck. A dog just followed her family home to stay. Isn't that a good sign? She is like her father and wasn't in favor of having a dog, but her kids and husband convinced her to keep Bruno. Wouldn't it be nice if we could wake up and find our pet walking up our driveway! Couldn't it just go like the story of Lily and Bruno, a free dog following us home from a walk or just showing up on our driveway?

Towards the end of writing this book, I dreamed we actually did get a dog and it was my husband who went and picked it out and brought it home to surprise me. I shared this final dream to put some more subtle pressure on him.

I was on a small hill and walked down to a puddle of water. Playing in that puddle was a small to medium dog with a dirty, blonde coat. It was a mixed breed of some kind and friendly. My husband was standing off to the side watching. Without words, we understood that it was in need of a home. In the next scene, he seems to be pleased that he has surprised me with a dog, the very dog we saw in the puddle that apparently needed a home. Wow, I think in my dream, he wants to do the guy thing and make me happy by getting me a dog—so sacrificial and charming. I realize it isn't hypo-allergenic and wonder how that will be.

I wake up and say to myself, now, that ain't gonna happen, no way. But what power can stop the combined effort of my active imagination and a wish fulfillment dream?

My Last Word

My husband will need persuading to get a dog. That is why I compiled a list of the top ten reasons everybody should get one. He seems to think living with a psychotherapist is a bit like living with a lawyer. And our friend Steve, who is also married to a psychotherapist, pointed out to him one night over dinner, "But you will never win an argument when you live with a shrink. He or she is always right."

Really! I thought law and therapy were two totally distinct and unrelated occupations! Nevertheless, here is my case for getting a dog:

1. **Unconditional love.**

2. **Always-available playmate.**

3. **Protector.** Whether real or imagined isn't the issue. It's a warm body for when you're scared.

4. **Meet and greeter.** Dogs are kind of like a welcome wagon to spread warmth and love in your home.

5. **Good for feng shui!** Dogs move energy, which helps release stagnation, something *feng shui* experts say is important for good *chi*.

6. **Exercise.** You have to walk the dog; it will get you outside.

7. **Practice "being."** Dogs seem to be able to do nothing and it somehow rubs off on you. You just get to relax naturally with them.

8. **Miracle workers.** Dogs know sometimes what you need even before you do. There are all kinds of savior stories with dogs.

9. **Fun!** Dogs love to play in the snow, roll in the grass or dirt, and hike in the woods.

10. **Our inner child.** Dogs bring out the inner child in all of us. And if that leads to greater warmth, connection, and healing, how can that not be a good thing?

On the other hand, let me help my husband. He thinks

a woman always has to have the last word. So let me surprise him. Here are the top ten reasons not to get a dog:

1. **Husband or dog?** I may get the dog but lose the husband in the process!

2. **Sharing a bathroom with Sophie.** Potty training is a lot of work.

3. **Psychosomatic illnesses.** Like Pepper, the poor dog will feel our pain.

4. **Life is already busy and full.** Don't bite off more than you can chew.

5. **Discipline and training.** It takes work. Have you ever watched one dog misbehave in a park? Not a pretty sight. Reminds one of how much really does go into training a dog. And you don't really know, especially if it's a puppy, what kind of dog you're going to get. Make sure you can look at birth order and the breeder's observations. But at the end of the day, it's like every relationship; you have ups and downs and have to find ways to work them through. Dogs don't talk back, but they don't cry either, so that's a mixed bag.

6. **They tie you down.** It's hard to be able to get up and go on vacation and travel especially on a moment's notice.

7. **Responsibility.** You have to take them to the vet if they are sick and feed them early in the morning even if you'd rather sleep in.

8. **Grief.** You will probably outlive the dog, so a goodbye is inevitable.

9. **Mess.** Shedding, accidents, smells, and the like come with dogs.

10. **Time commitment.** Especially the training part for discipline. You don't want to have to call a dog whisperer like Cesar Millan to come to your house. It's work training a dog. Didn't I already say this one? I'm back where I started . . . training, training, and more training.

This book is based on my personal reflections but informed by my professional experience. Animals, and I believe, dogs in particular, are great teachers. They are like wise old gurus. I almost said like saints, but that might be taking my Mitzie obsession a tad too far! I don't think she was particularly religious, anyway. And I've already told you what I think about dogs having souls.

Master Therapist Mitzie

There is a saying in Buddhism that goes something like this. "Look at the glass. It might be full; it might be half-empty. See the sun shining through it. It's beautiful. You can turn it around. And suddenly the glass falls and shatters. Celebrate the glass now while it is there." That is how I will look at having a dog should I ever be a part-time, full-time, semi-impermanent owner again. Dogs live in the present moment. I feel as if I am still in kindergarten when it comes to remembering this teaching. Be in the now.

Dogs provide real expertise on life, death, and rebirth. We are all on a journey and, in the process, share experiences, struggles, and victories. I'm a work-in-progress, and I invite my readers to take what is of interest to you. And if you are grieving the loss of a pet or hoping, like I am, to have a dog of your own, perhaps my story has shed light on your own pet cycle of life, death, and rebirth. I will be grateful for any benefit you find here as result of your interaction with what I had to say. We are all teachers and students.

Part IV

LIVING WITH LOSS

Honor Your Pet's Passing

"If you don't mind throwing tennis balls for eternity, I do have an opening in doggie heaven."

—*Frank and Ernest* comic strip: An angel at
St. Peter's gate, to a man seeking admittance

"The dog is a gentleman; I hope to go to his heaven, not man's."

—Mark Twain

his section shares pet loss tools and tips that can be helpful in identifying where you are in the grief process and ease the loss of a beloved pet. It has taken me over thirty years to create the rituals that would allow me to come to peace with our family pet's passing. Writing this grief memoir became a healing trip down memory lane reviewing favorite times with Mitzie and my rent a dogs. The readers guide questions is a tool that can help you heal your loss, too.

Being a Dog for a Day

After sharing so many stories with you, it is time to conclude with being more practical. It's never easy to lose a pet. This part has a set of pet loss tips and tools to cope with the loss of a beloved pet. You can choose for yourself; there are different tools for different people. Using the exercises can help ease the pain of your loss. It can be helpful in identifying where you are in the grief process and let you take steps to feel the grief and let go of a beloved pet.

But before you embark in this last part and follow my healing suggestions, let's have some fun and imagine to being a dog for a day. I thought of the idea of being a dog for the day when I went to get the morning paper one day. In the past, our neighbor's dog Brewster would usually come with me and even though he is long gone, I remember to this day turning the corner of the driveway with him by my side to greet the day. The sun would be rising in the east if it was a sunny day in Seattle. Brewster would always stop and sniff the air. On this particular morning I thought of him as I allowed myself a moment to stop and sniff the air as he would have done. I then thought *what would it be like if I did live a day as if I were looking through Brewster's eyes*. If I did the kinds of *living in the moment* activities only a dog would do.

If I were a dog I would.....

- Start by stretching my legs when I got up out of bed in the morning. You've seen dogs take those yoga poses they are named for, the downward dog pose for example.

- Greet my loved ones first thing in the morning and when they arrived or left the house

- Let them see the pure pleasure and joy showing on my face that they are in my life

- Take lots of walks, at least twice a day

- Go to the dog park to play and socialize

- Take a car ride with the windows down just because I love to feel the wind in my hair and smell the fresh air

- Play lots of Frisbee and ball

- Take a swim in a lake with abandon

- Explore nature and sniff every flower and blade of grass I come across

- Take a sunbath or two in the backyard

- Do nothing, just sit and be in the moment all day

- Let myself get good and bored realizing I have no responsibilities other than to love and be loved

- Sit and stare off into space a lot while still being alert at the same time

- Meditate a lot

- Eat only when I was hungry. No, I would not be eating dog food.

- Nap at least once a day

- Take a bike ride in my owner's bike basket or jogging stroller

- Be really present with others as a good companion

- Love others unconditionally

- Not hold any grudges because my memory is short

- Be intuitively alert when guests were coming up the driveway

- Take some quiet down time by myself in my bed during the day to recharge

- Yawn when I'm tired

- Chase a squirrel up a tree just because it's fun

- Curl up into a ball when I was ready to sleep without a care in the world

How do you feel now? Did you enjoy your day?

Preparing

Sometimes a pet's passing is unexpected, like in Maddie's accident. More often you can sense that your pet is coming near its time. Maybe you have visited a vet and heard the news from his mouth. In that case it helps to sit down and ask yourself some questions and make some preparations.

How to Decide

- How long have you had your dog?

- Does your dog play and still enjoy its usual activities?

- How is its appetite?

- What is your pet's level of play activity, quality of life, pain, discomfort, human interaction?

- Are there physical signs of stress: shivering, barking, panting, howling, growling, or whimpering?

- Is your pet's mobility affected? How about their sight or hearing, is it affected?

- Is your pet urinating involuntarily? Showing signs of weakness or vomiting?

- If your pet's health condition involves surgery will you pay for treatment or let go?

Create Sacred Space

How could you create a sacred space for a dying pet?

- If you believe in being greeted by loved ones who help you pass over, who do you think will be there to greet your pet when they pass over?

- What would you want around you if you were dying?

- Who would greet you?

- Would your pets be there waiting for you at the pearly gates?

Identify Where you are in the Grief Process

Bess Bailey, RN and MSN at the Connecticut Hospice offers the following six stages in the journey of grief that can help in recovering.

1. Loss, whether it is unexpected or you know it is coming can be devastating. The loss of a beloved pet can send you on a downward spiral.

2. Protest, here one goes through shock, numbness, confusion, anger and physical symptoms connected with the loss.

3. Searching, the mind and body may not fully have accepted the loss and are looking for answers about why it had to happen. For instance, exploring ideas around what happens to your pet when it dies. Why did he or she have to suffer or die in the middle of its prime?

4. Despair, agony, anguish, depression, slowed thinking and actions characterize this fourth phase, which is at the bottom of the grief decline.

5. Reorganization, bursts of energy, intermittent interest, indifference, fatigue, detachment and apathy all be a part of this adjustment period after the loss of a pet.

6. Reinvestment, coming to terms with the loss and feeling a sense of peace. Perhaps evaluating if you want to get another pet at this time in your life or deciding to just wait and see what life brings.

Grieving

Create an Inner Resource

As I mentioned earlier in the chapter on healing spaces, Eye Movement Desensitization and Reprocessing (EMDR), can be effectively used to heal loss. The therapy works with bi-lateral stimulation which creates new neuropathways in the brain. EMDR is a tool that can help you connect what you know with what you feel and ought be done with the help of a certified EMDR therapist. One of the components of EMDR is creating a safe, comforting resource.

Simply tapping the knee or shoulder is used to anchor a resource of comfort. Close your eyes and think of a beloved pet. Engage all of your senses: sight, sound, smell, touch, feeling, and the temperature in the room. With each hand, palms down, gently tap the top of each knee. Alternate back and forth at whatever pace feels comfortable. When you are ready, slowly open your eyes and come back into the room. You've tapped in your beloved pet as an inner resource. You may also try bi-lateral tapping by doing the butterfly. Just cross your arms across your chest your hands on your shoulders. Begin tapping your right and left shoulder, alternately back and forth while breathing deeply. When you are struggling with the loss of a pet, tapping in your pet ensures that their memory will always stay close to your heart. Tapping in your pet can also relax your body if its tense in stressful situations.

What happened when you tapped in your inner resource? Did you feel closer to a pet, either one who has passed over or one that is in your life right now? What are other resources to sooth, and comfort that you can tap in, such as a nurturing figure real or imaginary?

Create a Spirit Packet

I have a really great tip for coping with pet loss. Susan McElroy's book, *Why Buffalos Dance*, tells the story of creating a spirit packet after a beloved pet dies. She says to take some of the pet's objects and place them in a packet to put in a special place in or near the home. That way, every time you see that spirit pouch or packet, you will honor and remember your pet as you grieve and go through the process of letting go. Begin creating a spirit packet by taking some of your pets objects like a toy, a brush or a bowl and place them in a cloth packet in a special place in or near the home. This is especially helpful if your pet had health issues. When you see the packet you can remember the lively fun times rather than the painful, traumatic final moments.

On the anniversary of your pet's death, take the spirit packet and burn it. Releasing the ashes allows the spirit of your beloved animal, as well as your own, to move on.

Susan says she believes that our pets never really leave us. She feels that after the death of many of her own pets, she knows this to be true. It is important to grieve the passing of our pets so that we can give their spirits the full freedom they deserve. Pets come into our lives to hold the essence and energy that we are incapable of holding. Likewise, we humans also hold the essence or energy they are incapable of holding because they are of the animal kingdom. So we have this wonderful symbiotic relation-ship— animals and humans with each other. Each is holding essences the other can't. I felt this with Brewster's passing. Creating a spirit pouch or packet helps us in the grieving process to honor that symbiotic relationship.

I had never created a spirit packet, but was told about it after Brewster's death. So I went around the garage and yard picking up his plastic water bowl, food bowl, and toys. I then gave away his leftover treats and returned his spare bed in our garage to our neighbors. I took Brewster's doggie belongings and placed them in a bucket in our shed. Even though his things were gone memories of him lingered. When I sat on the patio I could clearly see in our line of bushes circling the patio square a squashed part of one of the bushes where he liked to lay his butt on the grass. "His" bush was considerably smaller than all the others. What could have been an annoyance was a now a fond memory of him spending time in our yard.

Create a Crying Container

There are many methods of grieving. Creating a dog memorial ceremony, watching sad movies, crafting memory photo albums and Facebook and Pinterest pages are just a few. In her book, *The Year of Magical Thinking,* Joan Didion suggests that grief is passive and mourning is active. Sometimes it helps to move through grief by creating a time and space to actively process loss. Creating a crying container is an active form of mourning. However, sitting home and crying alone all the time isn't a good idea. Mourning happens more easily with community and getting out and sharing the loss with others. Sometimes, it can be helpful to join a pet loss support group in person or online as a way to move beyond grief into active mourning.

As I mentioned earlier, I cry a lot more than the average person, I think, although I don't know the statistics. I can put on a tearjerker movie such as *Anne of Green Gables* if I ever need a good cry. The part where Matthew dies is heart wrenching. Other grief inducers are certain pieces of music that take me back to a memory, sitting in nature doing nothing, looking through picture albums, or sharing a story of a loved one that has passed on. For instance, I created my own dog memory photo book. Some of my family members loved it so much they asked me to make one for them. There are many ways to get into the grief zone but it isn't something that can be forced. It comes in waves all on its own.

Are you able to grieve about a lost pet? Sometimes an aura of mystery surrounds the ability to cry. It may just be bottled up inside and you can't find the release valve. Maybe your family, like mine, wasn't overly demonstrative when it came to tears. So how do you encourage the water faucet of tears? Here are some tips to create a healing space to work through your grief.

1. Turn on soft music, perhaps something that helps bring to mind fond memories of your pet.

2. Turn the lights down low.

3. Bring in some comforts like a cup of tea, a snack, and a blanket. Think the five senses here and see if you can create a mood invoking them. I like to warm up the room, light a candle, burn some incense, relax or hold a pillow, drink a cup of tea, or bring out a picture.

4. Remember the happy times with your pet. Think about your loss and drop that down into your heart.

5. Practice *Heartmath.org* by imagining you are breathing in and out from your heart for five breaths. (For more information, go to Appendix E, Suggested Web Links.)

6. If you like, write a journal about your pet.

7. Talk aloud to your pet if it feels right. Tell it how much you miss it and carry on a conversation as if it were right there beside you, almost feeling like you could reach out and touch its fur or feathers.

8. Make what I call an inner connection with yourself, your spirit, your soul. If you have a sense of God, a higher self, a guardian angel, an ancestor or an idea of all that is, connect and have a conversation.

9. Exercise and then take a warm bath or shower to relax before you settle into your space.

10. Just feel your feelings, remembering there is no right or wrong way to grieve. It all works.

11. Create a backyard memorial for your pet. I remember being together as a family and burying our pet turtle in our backyard. Flushing the gold fish down the toilet when it died was not an elaborate ritual by any means. We never had hamsters or gerbils so I imagine if we had, they would have been, buried alongside the turtle. As I mentioned, Mitzie dug up the dead turtle so that didn't exactly go as planned. Remember to go to my website, *www. lifedeathdog,* and download the free pet loss meditation that can help you feel better after your pet's passing.

Healing

Writing a letter

Write a letter to your pet telling it what it meant to you and how you will miss it. In the voice of your pet write a letter telling *what only my pet knows about me.*

Meditation

Find a quiet time when you won't be disturbed and take a moment to reconnect with the memory of your pet.

I invite you to take a journey within yourself to a place that feels like the very center of your being, that place where it's very quiet......and peaceful....and still. And when you're in that place....it's possible for you to reconnect with your beloved pet that has passed over. Images, thoughts, feelings, or bodily sensations may come to you about your pet. Maybe you would like to take a few moments of time to get in touch with the memory of your pet. The sights, smells, sounds, and the way their body felt in your hand warms your heart. What is a favorite pet memory of yours? Spend a few moments just being with the memories that drift and float up. Perhaps a time when you were feeling down that your pet was there to comfort you? Or a time that your pet made you laugh or play? Breathe in and center and just allow yourself to be with the memory of your pet.

Inhale deeply, a sense of freshness comes into your body. Know that your pet loved you. Reassure yourself you did okay, you did the best you could at the end of their life. If need be, let a wave of forgiveness pass through between you and your pet. You feel peaceful, you are grateful for your time together. Take three more deep breaths in and out and, when you are ready, slowly open your eyes, coming back into the room feeling refreshed and wide awake.

Heartmath Stress Reduction Technique

You can apply the freeze frame technique from *www.heartmath.org* to help with grief.

1. Recognize any stress and sad feelings around your pet's passing while taking a time out.

2. Shift your focus away from a racing mind or disturbed emotions to the area around your heart. Pretend you're breathing through your heart for ten seconds or more.

3. Recall a positive, fun feeling or time you've had in life with your pet and attempt to re-experience it.

4. Using your intuition, common sense and sincerity, ask your heart, what would be a more efficient response to the situation, one that would lessen stress and ease the grief?

5. Listen to what your heart says in answer to your question.

Ten Things You Can do to Take Your Mind Off Loss

1. Distract yourself by getting together with friends or going to the park. Do something your pet would have enjoyed.

2. Take a road trip and get out of town for the weekend.

3. Resume a hobby. Or if you don't have one, find one.

4. Volunteer to help someone less fortunate than you.

5. Dance your sorrows away.

6. Watch a favorite movie.

7. Do something physical, like cleaning the house.

8. Make a gratitude list.

9. Treat yourself to a massage.

10. Learn something new.

Ten Ways to Honor Your Pet on the Anniversary of His/Her Death

1. Look at old photos and home videos. Have a good cry or reminisce with family and friends.

2. Turn digital photos into an album on *canvas.com*.

3. Light a candle in honor of your pet with its picture.

4. Plant a tree, flower or bush to remember your pet by.

5. Plan a memorial service or candlelight vigil.

6. Reach out to Rainbow Bridge at *www.rainbow bridge.com* and light a virtual candle.

7. Print out a copy of the Rainbow Bridge poem and post it on your refrigerator.

8. Go to a favorite park or sit in your pet's favorite spot in your yard or house.

9. Take flowers to the grave, memorial site, or other place you go to remember your pet.

10. Burn a spirit packet for your pet.

Dreaming

Did you ever put a baby tooth under your pillow at night so the tooth fairy would bring you a quarter? (These days, it's gone up to $5 a tooth, I hear!) Instead of looking for the money, look for the dream to get you on your way. It may take days, weeks, even years, for those big night dreams to come, but if you don't look to your waking dreams and symbols for healing in your dreams you may be missing out on clues from your subconscious.

You need the right tools in order to record your dreams. A pen and paper or a digital recorder by your bed helps. I love the pens that come with an internal light. It's hard for the subconscious to think you are really serious about this whole dream stuff if you don't write things down. Just remember: You are not your dreams. Just because I dreamed that my family buys another Boston Terrier in a new house doesn't mean that we actually will get a Boston—or any other breed of dog, for that matter. But one can hope that it really is a dream that will come true!

There are other kinds of dreams. For instance:

1. Release dreams. These are like an emotional exhale, releasing anxiety and frustration. They may be nightmares and connected to cellular memories. Releasing is a safety valve, a letting go of emotional steam. Dreaming may reflect a theme like abandonment. Remember to change the end of the dream to a victory. For example, if you wake up in a house alone, go back to the dream and add people.

2. Information and problem-solving. Dreams can offer logical ideas that provide concrete solutions to problems you are facing in your life.

3. Wish dreams. These are simple, literal reflections of what you want or yearning memories such as soulful connections. Sigmund Freud suggested that dreams were an expression of "wish fulfillment."

4. Astral travel. This is flying without the benefit of

an airplane. It unfolds in a logical sequence of events like waking life; you may visit the deceased. Astral catalepsy is when the spirit has a hard time entering or exiting.

5. Precognition. These are hard to separate from the other dreams. If the information in the dreams turns out to be inaccurate, the dreams were undoubtedly either wish or release dreams. If the information turns out to be accurate, it could be precognitive and coming from the 'God,' the ancestral realm, or the higher self.

Dreams are an expression of your subconscious. Their meaning can be revealed in how you use them to understand yourself better. Wishes, fears, fantasies and anxieties are prime material for dreams. After you have had a dream what are the steps to analyzing it? Get a journal or piece of paper to record them.

Eleven Tips for Analyzing Your Dreams

1. Title it. By all means, give it a title and don't think too much about it. Whatever pops into your head is fine. You can always add a subtitle!

2. Look for themes. Look for a common thread or think of it as a melody that is repeated often in the dream. Jot these down under the title.

3. Draw a big circle. Identify the characters and images and put them all in their own separate little circles inside that big circle. Now draw two eyes and a mouth inside that big circle making a smiley face, because all those separate little parts are really a part of you.

4. Explore. Make free associations about each of those characters or images. For instance, if you have a dream about a deer, ask yourself, "What do deer symbolize to me?" Have you seen any lately? What were the circumstances? What comes to mind when you think of a deer?

5. Insight. Are there any past experiences similar with elements of the dream that stand out and are easy to make sense out of?

6. Share your dream with another. My husband also likes to analyze dreams, so if time permits and the dream appears, do that with another. Another possibility is to join a therapeutic dream process group.

7. Take time. Don't try to figure everything all out in one sitting. Let it percolate like a cup of coffee.

8. Watch for symbol synchronicities. Look for random coincidental events that seem related to but aren't really caused by the other.

9. Practice. It takes commitment to record those dreams down and practice analyzing them.

10. Seek feedback. Ask others to listen to or read your dream and then respond as *if it were their dream.* Remember: You always get the last word so you can reclaim your dream.

11. Take action. If the dream gives clear clues to help you implement a decision, take action. Ask for a dream before you fall asleep so you can get help with whatever ails you.

Appendix A

CAST OF MASTER THERAPISTS

Cast of Master Therapists

I've for the most part used the original pet names. I'm sure they won't sue me for doing so. For that matter, all but Sophie are not among us anymore. A few dogs are mentioned whose names I can't remember, but believe me, there is a reason why I can't remember! I wish I still had that book of dog stamps I had growing up (there is a bit of a pack rat beyond nostalgic in me, after all) because I have no idea what breed some of these master therapist dogs are. So to all the dogs I've loved before and that have gone before me, if I have mistaken you for the wrong breed or mix, please forgive me.

Alvin	Rose's childhood dog
Bernie	Saint Bernard on my mom's farm
Brewster	Neighbor's German Shepherd
Bridget	Rent-a-dog yellow Lab
Buffy	Childhood neighbor's Collie-type dog
Buster	Mother's farm dog
Coco	Friend's Maltese dog
Cooper	Parents' rent-a-dog golden Lab and German Shepherd mix
Dash	Oreo's blond Havenese brother
Fluffy	Nursing home cat
Healthcliff	Connie's childhood Yorkie
Jazz	Colleague's black Lab
Jeb	Mother's farm Saint Bernard
Joker	Childhood neighbor's dog
Kaylee	Sottish Terrier honorary rent-a dog
Lily	White cat on the flower farm

Maddie	Maltese dog on the road
Mitzie	Boston Terrior from childhood
Oreo	Dash's black-and-white Havenese brother
Oscar	Roommate's pet parakeet
Pedro	Husband's childhood pet Poodle
Porter	Parents' rent-a-dog black Lab
Scruffy	Rose's grandfather's dog
Shep	Mother's farm dog #2
Sophie	Dash's younger blonde Havenese sister

Appendix B

GLOSSARY

Glossary

This book is based on my personal reflections and uses some therapeutic terms that I will try to explain simply here, along with some personal terms I have invented:

Archetypes
Universal ideas, images, symbols and patterns common to all.

Boston Terriers
The best breed of dog ever.

Client-centered therapy
A form of therapy developed by Carl Rogers that is non-directive and reflective. It trusts that the client has his or her own innate wisdom.

Collective unconscious
C. G. Jung's term for a deep, inherited unconscious where dreams, memories and everything that ever happened are in an unconscious shared by all.

Countertransference
Transference was a word coined by Sigmund Freud to label the way patients "transfer" feelings from important persons in their early lives, onto the psychoanalyst or therapist. In countertransference, the therapist is transferring feelings onto a client. Countertransference, most of the time, is not always helpful. Particularly when it is unexamined—or, worse, unrecognized—it can indeed interfere with a client's therapy.

EMDR
Eye movement desensitization and reprocessing (EMDR) uses a patient's own rapid, rhythmic eye move-

ments. These eye movements dampen the power of emotionally charged memories of past traumatic events.

Empathy

Understanding the emotions and feelings of another, perhaps without being articulated out loud.

Genuineness

A sincere, real, true presence with nothing artificial.

Humanistic psychology

Founded by Abraham Maslow, this third force after psychoanalytic and behaviorism concerns itself with human motives and self-development.

Impermanence

A principle in Buddhism suggesting that all in life is not permanent or enduring, but fleeting. It is temporary and will only last for so long.

Jung, Carl Gustav

A Swiss psychotherapist who founded analytical psychology. Jung proposed and developed the two concepts of extroversion and introversion, archetypes, and the collective unconscious.

Letter of apology

Something I wrote to my dog twenty years after she had died to help both Mitzie and I, to move on and to say I'm sorry I wasn't as always as compassionate as I could have been.

Part-time dog

A dog that has come into your life for a short period to which you quickly grow attached and consider it as if it were your ow—temporarily, that is.

Psychosomatic pains
Pains that are assumed to have at least part cognitive and emotional psychological basis.

Rayner, Ray
He had his own children's television show based in Chicago, Illinois, and featuring Bozo's Circus. Bozo was a clown children adored.

Rent-a dog
A dog that you borrow from another because your life-style doesn't afford you the opportunity to have one yourself. Or you don't think you could live with the guilt of leaving a dog behind when you aren't home.

Repetition compulsion
A compulsion that is irrational or an irresistible desire to repeat some behavior.

Rogerian
A buzz word for Carl Roger's therapy approach to helping others.

Shrine
A holy place, a place to celebrate life, death, and rebirth that can remain undisturbed for years.

Suffering
In Buddhism, all is suffering. It is one of the four noble truths suggesting that suffering comes ultimately from our mind and is a desire to seek permanence or recognize the self when neither can exist.

Totem animal
Among native people, an animal or natural object takes on a symbol of meaning for an individual, family or clan.

Transference

Attempting to complete with new people, places, pets and things what is still incomplete in your past.

Vulnerability

That which is sensitive to or open to injury or wounding.

Yang

In Chinese philosophy, the male principle or force.

Yin

In Chinese philosophy, the feminine principle or force.

APPENDIX C

TERRA DONA PUBLISHING READING GROUP GUIDE

Terra Dona Publishing
Reading Group Guide

for
Life, Death, Dog
by
Karen Hansen

The questions, discussion topics and reading list are intended to enhance insights in yourself or discussions with others. Use Journal Questions to remember and celebrate the lives of your pets.

Part I—LIFE: DOGS ARE MASTER THERAPISTS

Empathy

- How does your pet show you unconditional love?

- What life lessons have you learned from pets?

Genuineness

- Was your pet more attached to some members of your family?

- Was it because they fed it?

- How did your pet take care of you if you had a bad day?

- What pet rituals did you have with your pet?

- Any special way you started the day together?

- Are there pet rituals that have been passed down through the generations?
- What lasting impressions stay with you about your pet in this world or the next?

Unconditional Positive Regard

- How did you come to own your beloved pet?
- If you picked it out of a litter, what was special about your pet that made you chose it? What are your fondest memories with your pet?
- Did you always know that you would have a dog chapter with your partner?
- How did you decide if you should get a dog as a family?

First Mitzie Dream

- Do you ever dream of your pet?
- Review the five dreams in the book, First Mitzie dream, "Mitzie in the Forest,": Second Mitzie Dream, "Burying her Brush,": Third Mitzie Dream, "Just One More Walk Around the Block,": Fourth Mitzie dream, "Visiting My Parents and a Boston in Heaven"; and "Final Dream."
- Reflect on any dreams you have had about your pet.
- Have you ever looked at each part of your dream as representing a part of yourself?

Part-Time Pets are the Best

- Have you ever petsat for someone?

- What would make a good part-time pet?

- If you haven't already read the book, Part-Time dog by Jane Thayer.

- Ever taken home a stray animal?

Pancakes

Ponder all of your firsts with your pet, for example, your pet's first car ride.

- Vacation

- Holiday

- Toy

- Scare

- Pouting episode

- Guilty look

- Friend in the neighborhood

- Food strike

- Visit to the vet, kennel, doggie daycare, or obedience class

- Overnight stay away from home

- Dressup for Halloween, Christmas or just for fun

- Time they did something that made you laugh so hard you cried

- Time they ran off the yard or away from the house

- Episode of swallowing something it shouldn't have

- Person or animal they didn't take a liking to

- Look that won you over after they did something they shouldn't have

- Illness
- Medicine

Grounding With Your Pets

- How does your pet help you keep both feet on the ground?
- Are you active with your pet whether it is playing tug of war or walking outside?
- Has your pet ever come to your rescue?

Intuition and Pets

- How has your pet kept you company when you were sick?
- Have you ever noticed that your pet just naturally knows when you need some tender loving care or when you have had a bad day?
- Does your pet just seem to know when to stay close, lick your hand, jump up for lap time or comfort you in other ways?

Laughter is the Best Medicine

- What is the funniest thing your pet has ever done?
- What is the most mischievous thing your pet has ever done? For instance, snuck off the couch when you came home, slept in or on your bed?
- How does your pet act like a human?
- Do they ever try to run the show around the house?

- Does your pet sleep in your bedroom? On your bed? Under the covers? On your pillow? Does your pet take over and have more space in your bed than you do?

Healing Spaces

- What do you see when you look into your pet's eyes?
- How is your pet a healing space for you?

Pet Transference

- Can you imagine or see how transference happens in your life in regard to your pet?
- How is your pet a source of safety or security in your life?

PART II—DEATH: IN BETWEEN PETS

Unfinished Mourning

- When did you first notice that your pet was aging or something wasn't right about your pet?
- How did your family cope with the loss of your pet?
- What are your family's reactions to grief in general?
- How does grief manifest for you?

- Are you nostalgic?

- Do you have any keepsakes of your pets?

- How do you let go of the past in order to make room for new starts?

Hard Losses

- Do you have a favorite animal movie?

- Did you have to make a decision about medical care or surgery for your pet?

- What was that like?

- Were you able to say goodbye to your pet or was its death sudden and unexpected?

- Did your pet die at home, or did you drive it to your vet or have a mobile vet come to the home?

- Have you had to make a hard choice to euthanize a pet?

- If you had to put down your pet, what was that decision like for you and your family?

Psychic Pet Dreams

- What were your first experiences with death?

- Have you had a psychic pet dream?

- Why do you think the woman in the lecture series had a series of dreams in which a family member died prematurely?

- Do the heavens prepare us for loss?

Goodbye to Brewster

- Have you been with a pet when it has passed over?

- If you were given the opportunity, what special things would you do with or for your pet before his/her passing?

- If you have kids, how do you talk to them about the loss?

Maltese on the Road

- What did you observe and learn from the moment of being with a pet when it passed over?

- What are comforting and supportive words to say to someone or a pet who is passing over? What can you say to a child to comfort him or her?

- What are some not-so-sensitive things that people say when a pet passes over?

- What do you think it meant that Maddie had crossed the author and her sister's path?

More Passings

- Did you walk around the house the first day in a daze after your pet's passing expecting your pet to be around the corner?

- If you have other pets, what was it like for them?

- What are your beliefs about what happens after death?

- Do you have ways to grieve?

- If you are looking for ways to ease the loss of a pet,

consider creating a crying container as described in this section.

The Cycle of Life

- What personal encounters have you had with animals in the wildlife? How did they affect you?
- Have you over-played the role of rescuer towards a pet, wildlife or human?
- Have you witnessed an animal's suffering at the end of life?
- Where and when have you witnessed the cycle of life, death, and rebirth?

Second Mitzie Dream

- Did your pet have a favorite spot outside?
- The brush and deer were symbolic messages associated with her pet for the author. Do you have any symbolic messages about your pet?
- How do you remember and record your dreams?

Brewster's Graduation

- Did your pet provide a protective presence?
- Was it in any way a fierce companion?

Pet Visitations

- Have you ever had or known someone who had a pet visitation?

- Are you open to such an experience?
- Do you believe former pets come back to aid the dying in passing over?
- Where do you think pets go when they die?
- What do you think happens to animals in the afterlife?
- What happens when people die?
- Is death the same or different as for people with pets and animals?

Ashes to Ashes

- Who will be in your welcome wagon at your death bed?
- Do animals have a soul?

Memorabilia

- Do you have pet paraphernalia?
- What are the stages of grief we go through according to Kubler Ross?
- If you lost a pet as a child what are the stages of grief you went through?
- How many ways can you eulogize a dog?

Memorials

- What do you think of the past ritual of taking a family memorial photograph with a deceased pet?
- Do you have any pictures or mementos of your

pet? Use the space below to insert a picture of your pet.

- How did you memorialize your pet?

Angel Wings

- How can you tap into your pet's memory?

- If you had your pet cremated what did you do with the ashes?

Insert a picture of your pet here

A Letter of Apology

Writing a letter of apology is a great way to bring to mind memories from the past and memorialize your beloved pet. If you have any regrets, you can voice them and put them to peace in the past.

Explore writing a letter of apology to your pet. Take a trip down memory lane and record some memories.

- Do you have a favorite memory of your pet?

- What were your pet's favorite activities?

- What was your pet's personality like?

- What would you like to say that would bring you a greater sense of peace around your pet's passing?

- Are you harboring any guilty feelings from the loss of your pet that you need to let go of?

Third Mitzie Dream

- Have you had any pet dreams?

Rest in Peace

- Is your pet that passed over now a totem animal for you?

- How did your pet embody Carl Roger's humanistic psychology principles of empathy, genuineness and unconditional positive regard?

- What have your early experiences of the death of a pet taught you about loss and dying?

PART III—DOG: THE NEXT DOG OR NOT?

Waking Dreams

Use the "if it were my dream" technique to begin interpreting a dream with another.

Inner Child

- Do you have any hidden grief around pets that you need to share?

- Which of the four inner child archetypes: the inner child, the universal child, the innocent and the orphan do you identify with?

- Is your pet a gateway to any of these four inner children?

Fourth Mitzie Dream

- Have you had any dreams that helped you put your pet's memory to rest?

- What synchronicities have you experienced in your life?

Dreaming of Dogs—Again

- Are you dog-less, single with a dog, or with partner and a dog?

- What are the big decisions in deciding to get a dog?

- If you live with others how do you decide to let in a pet?

Is a Dog Man's Best Friend?

- Is your pet more attached to one member of the family than another?

- What are the advantages and disadvantages of getting a dog?

- Do you believe that pets can heal?

- Do you believe that pets can take on an owner's aches and pains?

- Do you know any pets that were natural healers?

- What are your thoughts and feelings about getting a dog for protection?

Reality and Relationship

- How do you take into consideration different needs and thoughts about getting a pet?

- What do you think of bringing a pet home unannounced to an unsuspecting family member?

- What compromises are possible when considering adding a pet to the family?

- Do you really need a dog chapter in your family?

- If you have a partner, how do you decide together whether or not to get a dog?

- If one partner would feel imposed upon to care for a dog, discuss how their boundaries could be respected where the dog is concerned. Perhaps look into where in your partner's past they were triggered.

- When was your partner the "dumpee" of another's responsibility in the home?

- Where was it difficult for them to set boundaries and have them respected without consequences?
- When were their needs low on the totem pole in a household?
- Have you ever seen a pet triangulate a couple before?
- In retirement do you want pets?

For Better and for Worse

- What do you think women want?
- Do you think women are looking for sovereignty as the Arthurian legend suggests?
- Is that fair in a relationship?
- Does it make for a healthy, balanced, equal relationship?

Dogs with Tears

- How are the roles changing between men and women today?
- How does the current cultural, political and social system fit today's women?
- Are pets and partners interchangeable?
- Do pets and partners compete?
- Do you believe having a pet makes a couple and or a family's life richer?
- In what way do you agree or disagree?
- Do dogs have emotions?
- Do you think dogs cry?

- What is your experience of having others feel your pain and cry with you?

- What are the differences between human and pet empathy?

Doggie Decisions

- Would getting another Boston Terrier be a good idea for the author?

- What kinds of dog breeds do you like?

- Do you want a little or a big dog?

- Is the human-to-pet ratio evident in your household?

- Do you have more than one child? In that case, would you consider getting more than one dog?

- Does anyone in the family have animal allergies? Are they mild or severe? Consider using NAET, Natural Allergy Elimination Therapy, Tapas acupressure technique or allergy shots to treat allergic reactions.

- Should the dog be hypo-allergenic?

- Have you ever been to a dog show?

Puppies, Training, Gender and Cats

- What are your thoughts and experiences about training a dog?

- Do you want a puppy or not?

- What are the pros and cons to getting a mature dog versus a puppy?

- What kind of dog personality or temperament fits your household?

- Do you want a male or female pet?

- Do you like dogs or cats better or both?

Active Imagination

- What are the joys and struggles of being a pet parent?

- Do you treat your pet like a little human sometimes?

- How do you decide to get another pet or not?

- Or do you just decide I'm not up for another dog chapter now or maybe never again?

- How long do you wait to get another pet? A month, year?

- How do you know a pet isn't being used to fill an empty void or unhealed grief for the death of a former pet or person?

- Does the next pet ever surpass the memory of a previous pet?

- Do you ever use visualization in your life to manifest your hopes, dreams and goals?

- What are the limits of pet therapy when it comes to emotional intimacy?

My Last Word

- What are your top reasons to get or not get a dog?

- How are you celebrating the now with or without a pet?

- Who would you say has the last word in your house?

APPENDIX D

SUGGESTED BOOKS ON HEALING GRIEF

Suggested Books on Healing Grief

The Year of Magical Thinking by Joan Didion

The Complete Dream Book: Discover What Your Dreams Reveal about You and Your Life by Gillian Holloway

Healing Grief and *Talking to Heaven* by James Van Praagh, Audio Recordings

The Courage to Grieve by Judy Tatelbaum

Good Grief by Granger Westberg

The Shack by William P. Young

APPENDIX E

SUGGESTED WEB LINKS

Suggested Web Links

www.griefshare.org – 12-part film series on grieving

www.vetmed.wsu.edu/PLHL/ – Pet Loss Hotline 1-(866) 266-8635 or (509) 335-5704. A group of Washington state university veterinarian students who have been trained by a licensed therapist in grief counseling

www.petloss.com

www.rainbowbridge.com

www.aplb.org – Association for pet loss and bereavement

www.aspca.com – Association for the prevention of the cruelty to animals

www.humanesociety.org

www.lightning-strike.com

www.petlossmessageboard.com

www.heartmath.org

www.counseling.org – for guidelines on animal assisted therapy

www.humanesociety.org

Endnotes

1   James Baraz, *Awakening Joy: 10 steps to Happiness.* (New York: Bantam, 2010), 98.

2   David Richo. *When the Past Becomes the Present: Healing the Emotional Wounds That Sabotage Our Relationships* (New York: Shambhala, 2008), 61.

3   David Richo, *When the Past Becomes the Present: Healing the Emotional Wounds That Sabotage Our Relationships* (New York: Shambhala, 2008), 138.

4   Kevin Todeschi and Henry Reed, "Dreaming for guidance," *Venture Inward*, October-December 2014, 49-52.

5   Elizabeth Kubler-Ross, *On Death and Dying* (New York: Scribner, 1997), 12.

6   C. G. Jung in his introduction to W. Y. Evans-Wentz, *The Tibetan Book of the Dead* (New York: Oxford University Press, 1960), xlvii.

7   Joan Walsh, "Good Eye: Interview with Ken Burns." *San Francisco Focus.* KQED via Online-Communicator.com. Archived from the original on September 22, 2011.

8   Diane Kennedy Pike, Life is a Waking Dream: *How to Explore your Most Vivid Experiences and Find Meaning Within Them* (New York: Riverhead Books, 1997), 264.

9   John Schwartz, "Big Boys Don't Cry, Do They?" *New York Times*, January 2, 2011, ST2, 200.

10   Adolf Guggenbhul-Craig, *Marriage: Dead or Alive* (New York: Spring, 2001), 76.

About the Author

KAREN HANSEN, PhD, LMHC is a psychotherapist and coach blending spirituality with a Jungian transpersonal perspective. In her work it is her goal to help people realize their abilities so that they can start living their life to its full potential. She has witnessed many people coming to therapy who need to grieve the loss of a pet. Karen lives in the Pacific Northwest.

www.lifedeathdog.com
www.transpersonaltherapy.com
www.ourladyfaces.com

(425) 361-3908

Made in the USA
San Bernardino, CA
07 June 2016